Junior NKIERE MAKOLONI

Information and communication techniques course 4th year

Junior NKIERE MAKOLONI

Information and communication techniques course 4th year

Scientific humanities

ScienciaScripts

Imprint
Any brand names and product names mentioned in this book are subject to trademark, brand or patent protection and are trademarks or registered trademarks of their respective holders. The use of brand names, product names, common names, trade names, product descriptions etc. even without a particular marking in this work is in no way to be construed to mean that such names may be regarded as unrestricted in respect of trademark and brand protection legislation and could thus be used by anyone.

Cover image: www.ingimage.com

This book is a translation from the original published under ISBN 978-3-639-62157-0.

Publisher:
Sciencia Scripts
is a trademark of
Dodo Books Indian Ocean Ltd. and OmniScriptum S.R.L publishing group

120 High Road, East Finchley, London, N2 9ED, United Kingdom
Str. Armeneasca 28/1, office 1, Chisinau MD-2012, Republic of Moldova, Europe
Managing Directors: Ieva Konstantinova, Victoria Ursu
info@omniscriptum.com

Printed at: see last page
ISBN: 978-620-8-51713-7

Contents

SUMMARY

Our aim in writing this book for students in the fourth year of Humanities is to support the national curriculum for this option, which is rich in Information and Communication Technologies (ICT). In this book, we have developed concepts related to computer networks, social networks, client-server systems, artificial intelligence and other concepts based on different algorithms. We have used the national curriculum for the year 2021 as the basis for the book.

It should also be noted that this book is written with a great deal of courage and love in order to raise the level of knowledge of our science option students and bring up to standard our ICT teachers who have not been able to tackle their computer studies up to degree level.

CHAPTER I

COMPUTER NETWORKS

1.1. GENERAL INFORMATION ON COMPUTER NETWORKS

I.1.1.DEFINITION

A computer network is a collection of equipment linked together to exchange information.

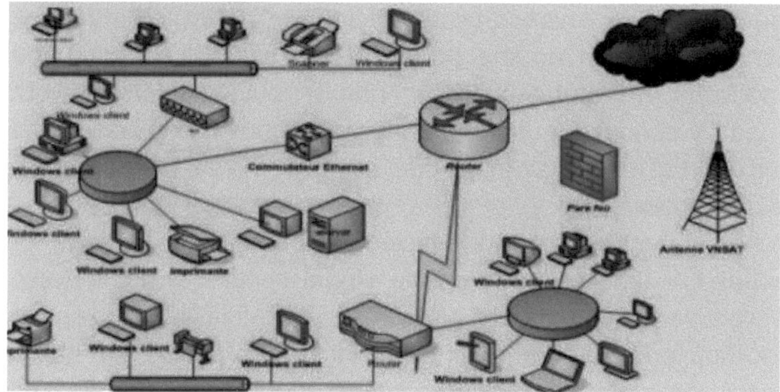

I.1.2.NETWORK EQUIPMENT

The most commonly used network equipment is as follows:

- Hub

. Switch

- Router
- Bridge
- Gateway

. Modem

- Repeater

. Access point

HUB

Concentrators connect several items of computer network equipment. A concentrator also acts as a repeater, amplifying signals that deteriorate after travelling long distances on the connecting cables. The concentrator is the simplest of the family of network connection devices, as it connects LAN components with identical protocols.

A concentrator can work with both digital and analogue data, provided that its parameters are configured in such a way as to prepare the incoming data for formatting. If, for example, the incoming data is in digital format, the concentrator must transmit it as packets; but if the incoming data is analogue, the concentrator transmits it as a signal.

Hubs do not perform packet filtering or addressing functions; they simply send data packets to all connected devices. Hubs operate at the physical layer of the Open Systems Interconnection (OSI) model. There are two types of concentrator: single-port and multi-port.

SWITCH

Switches generally play a more intelligent role than hubs. A switch is a multi-port device that improves network efficiency. The switch manages limited routing information on the nodes of the internal network and allows connections to systems such as hubs or routers. Local network trunks are usually connected using switches. Switches can usually read the physical addresses of incoming packets and forward them to the appropriate destination.

Using switches improves network efficiency compared with hubs or routers, because of their ability to create virtual circuits. Switches also improve network security, as virtual circuits are more difficult to examine with network monitors. You can think of a switch as a device that has a combination of some of the most interesting capabilities of routers and hubs. A switch can operate either on the Data Link layer or on the Network layer of the OSI model. A multilayer switch is a switch that can operate on both layers, meaning that it can be used as both a switch and a router. A multilayer switch is a high-performance device that supports the same routing protocols as routers.

Switches are susceptible to Distributed Denial of Service (DDoS) attacks; saturation attack prevention systems are used to prevent malicious traffic from stopping the switch. Switch port security is important, so make sure you secure your switches: Disable all unused ports and use DHCP snooping, ARP inspection and MAC address filtering.

ROUTER

Routers help to transmit packets to their destinations by tracing a path through the ocean of interconnected network equipment, using different network topologies. Routers are intelligent devices that store information about the networks to which they are connected. Most routers can be configured to work as packet filtering firewalls and use access control lists (ACLs). Routers, in conjunction with a Channel Service Unit/Data Service Unit (CSU/DSU), are also used to translate LAN rasterisation into WAN rasterisation. This is necessary because local area networks (LANs) and wide area networks (WANs) use different protocols. Such routers are called border routers. They provide the external connection from a local network to a wide area network, and they operate at the

border of your network.
Routers are also used to split internal networks into two or more sub-networks. It is also possible to connect internal routers to other routers, to create areas that operate independently of each other. Routers establish communication by managing tables of destinations and local connections. A router contains information on the systems connected to it and on the destination of requests to be sent if this is not known. Routers generally communicate routing and other information using one of three standard protocols: Routing Information Protocol (RIP), Border Gateway Protocol (BGP) or Shortest Path First Open (OSPF).
Routers are your first line of defence and should be configured so that only traffic authorised by network administrators is transmitted. The routings themselves can be configured as static or dynamic. If they are static, they can only be configured manually and remain so until they are changed. If they are dynamic, routers learn about the other routers in their environment and use information about them to build their routing tables.
Routers are universal devices that interconnect two or more heterogeneous networks. They are generally dedicated to specialised computers and have separate input and output network interfaces for each connected network. Since routers and gateways form the backbone of large computer networks such as the Internet, they have special characteristics that give them the flexibility and ability to adapt to different network addressing systems and frame sizes by segmenting large packets into smaller ones, adapted to the new network components. Each router interface has its own address resolution protocol (ARP), its own LAN address (network card address) and its own IP address (Internet protocol). The router, thanks to a routing table, knows the routes that a packet can take from its source to its destination. The routing table, like the bridge and switch, develops dynamically. On receiving a packet, the router removes its header and *trailer,* then analyses the IP header, determining the source and destination addresses and the type of data, and noting the time of reception. It also updates the routing table with new addresses that are not already there. The IP header and time-of-arrival information are entered into the routing table. Routers normally operate at the Network layer of the OSI model.

BRIDGE

Bridges are used to connect two or more hosts or network segments. The fundamental role of bridges in network architecture is to store and transfer frames between the different segments they connect. They use the MAC (medium access control) addresses of the equipment to transfer frames. By examining the MAC address of the devices connected to each segment, bridges can transmit data or prevent it from crossing. Bridges can also be used to connect two physical LANs into a larger logical LAN.

Bridges only work at the Physical and Data Link layers of the OSI model. Bridges are used to divide large networks into smaller sections by placing themselves between two physical network segments and managing the flow of data between the two.

Bridges are similar to hubs in many ways, including the fact that they connect LAN components with identical protocols. However, bridges filter incoming data packets, called frames, according to their addresses before transmitting them. While filtering data packets, bridges make no changes to the format or content of incoming data. Bridges filter and transfer frames in the network using a dynamic bridge table. This bridge table, which is initially empty, manages the LAN addresses of each computer on the local network and the addresses of each bridge interface linking the local network to other local networks. Bridges, like hubs, can be single port or multiple port.

Bridges have largely fallen into disuse in recent years and have been replaced by switches, which offer more functionality. In fact, switches are sometimes called "multi-port bridges" because of the way they work.

GATEWAY

Gateways generally operate at the Transport and Session layers of the OSI model. At the Transport layer and above, numerous protocols and standards from different suppliers are used; gateways are used to manage them. Gateways provide the translation between network technologies such as Open Systems Interconnection (OSI) and TCP/IP (Transmission Control Protocol/Internet Protocol). Thus, gateways connect two or more autonomous networks, each with its own routing algorithms, protocols, topology, domain name service, network administration procedures and policies.

Gateways perform all the functions of routers and more. In fact, a router with additional translation functionality is a gateway. The function that translates between different network technologies is called a protocol converter.

MODEM

Modems (modulator-demodulators) are used to transmit digital signals over analogue telephone lines. The digital signals are therefore converted by the modem into analogue signals of different frequencies and transmitted to another modem at the receiving end. The receiving modem performs the reverse transformation and provides a digital output to the device connected to it, usually a computer. The digital data is usually transferred to/from the modem via a serial link and a standard RS-232 interface. Many telephone companies offer DSL services and many cable operators use modems as end terminals for identification and recognition of individual users. Modems operate at both the Physical and Data Link layers.

REPEATER

A repeater is an electronic device that amplifies the signal it carries. You can think of a repeater as a device that carries a signal and retransmits it at a higher level or power , so that it can cover longer distances, more than 100 metres for standard LAN cables. Repeaters operate on the physical layer.

ACCESS POINT

Although an access point can technically include a wired or wireless connection, it is generally a wireless device. An access point operates at the second OSI layer, the Data Link layer, and can function either as a bridge connecting a standard cable network to wireless devices or as a router transmitting data from one access point to another.

Wireless access points (WAPs) consist of a transmitter and a receiver, which are used to create a wireless local area network (WLAN). Access points are generally separate pieces of network equipment with an integrated antenna, transmitter and adapter. Access points use the wireless infrastructure network mode to provide a connection point between wireless local area networks (WLANs) and a cabled Ethernet local area network. They also have multiple ports, allowing you to extend the network to support additional clients. Depending on the size of the network, one or more access points may be required to ensure complete coverage. Additional APs allow access to more wireless clients and extend the reach of the wireless network. Each access point is limited by its transmission range: the distance a client can be from the access point and still get a usable signal and data processing speed. The actual distance depends on the wireless standard, obstacles and environmental conditions between the client and the access point. Top-of-the-range access points are equipped with high-power antennas, which enable them to extend the range of the wireless signal.

Access points can also provide a large number of ports to increase the size of the network, the capacity of the firewall and the DHCP (Dynamic Host Configuration Protocol) service. So we have access points that are simultaneously a switch, a DHCP server, a router and a firewall.

To connect to a wireless access point, you need an SSID (Service Set Identifier). 802.11 wireless networks use the SSID to identify all systems belonging to the same network, and client workstations must be configured with the SSID to be authenticated by the access point. The access point can broadcast the SSID, which allows all wireless clients in the area to see its SSID. However, for security reasons, access points can be configured not to broadcast the SSID, which means that an administrator must give the SSID to client systems instead of allowing it to be discovered automatically. Wireless devices are shipped with default SSIDs, default security settings, default channels, default passwords and default user names. For security reasons, it is strongly recommended that you change these settings as soon as possible, as many websites list manufacturers' default settings.

Access points can be "light" or "heavy". Heavy

access points, also known as standalone access points, must be manually

manually configured with network and security parameters;

they then operate largely on their own and serve customers

until they can no longer function. Lightweight access points

can be configured remotely using a controller. As thin clients do not need to be manually configured, they can be easily reconfigured and monitored. Access points can be dependent on a controller or standalone.

NB: A good knowledge of the types of network equipment available will enable you to design and build a secure network that is well suited to your organisation. However, to ensure that your network remains secure and available at all times, you need to keep a close eye on your network equipment and the activities that affect it, in order to detect hardware or configuration problems and attacks quickly.

1.1.3. ROLES OF COMPUTER NETWORKS

The role of the IT network is first and foremost to act as a platform for sharing data and software resources between all the members of a company. A function that may seem basic today, but without which it would be impossible to function optimally.

Unlike two computers connected by a cable, modern networks are increasingly complex. Above a certain number of users, a server is used as a central point to distribute resources to all the computers on the premises. This is a client/server configuration. As well as sharing data and resources, it is now used to facilitate management, backup and storage, as well as setting the various rights for security.

The need for a well-functioning network means that experts in this field are of vital importance to companies of all sizes. That's why they're always in such demand on the job market.

1.1.4. NETWORK TYPES

To classify computer networks, a classification criterion must first be clearly defined. In this section we will classify them according to size. The diagram below illustrates the classification of computer networks according to size.

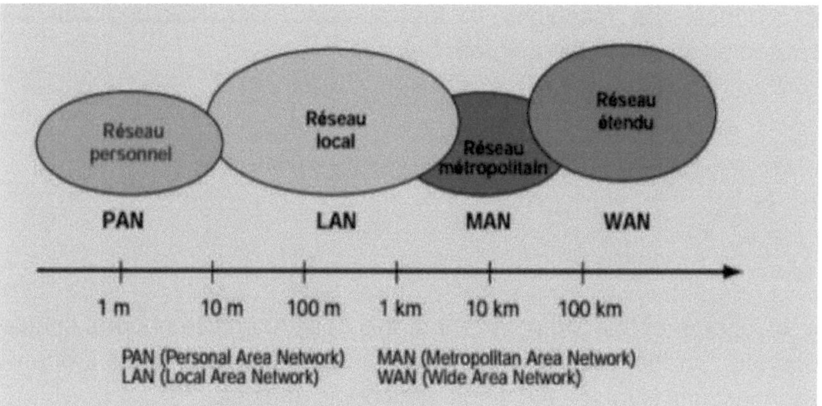

We can then classify them as follows:

- **The PAN** (Personale Area Network) refers to the very small network of some size used to interconnect personal machines, in particular laptops, mobile phones, telephones...
- **LANs** (Local Area Networks) are networks adapted to the size of a site, with the two furthest points no more than 1 km apart. These are sometimes referred to as corporate local area networks.
- **The MAN** (Metropolitan Area Network) is the interconnection of local networks. It is also often referred to as a regional network. The size (maximum distance) is generally of the order of 10Km;
- **The WAN** (Wade Area Network) refers to distances of several hundred or thousand kilometres linking IT equipment across a country, a continent or an entire planet.

1.1.5. NETWORK TOPOLOGIES

Topology refers to the fapon whose network equipment is interconnected via the communication media and the fapon whose information circulates in the network.

Two topologies are distinguished:

- **Physical topology**: How is equipment physically interconnected?
- **Logical topology**: how does data pass through the communications media? Physical topology Several physical topologies can be identified:

I. PHYSICAL TOPOLOGY

A. BUS TOPOLOGY

A bus topology is the simplest way of organising a network. In this topology, all the computers are connected to the same transmission line via a cable, usually coaxial. The word "bus" refers to the physical line that connects the machines in the network. This topology can be illustrated as shown in the diagram below.

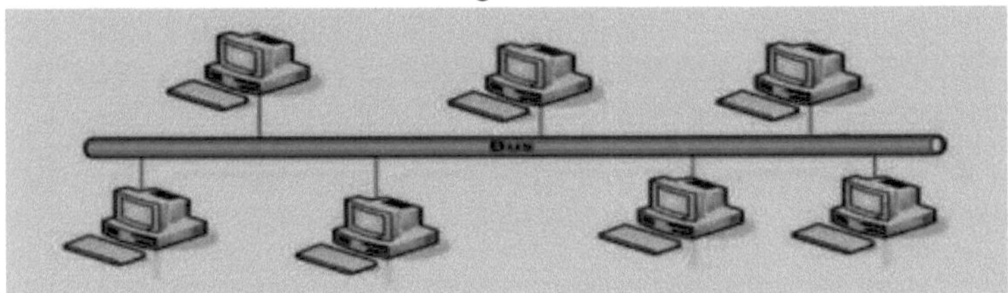

The advantage of this topology is that it is easy to implement and simple to operate. On the other hand, it is extremely vulnerable, since if one of the connections is faulty, the whole network is affected.

B. STAR TOPOLOGY

In this topology, the computers and other network equipment are connected to a central hardware system called a distribution frame. This is a box containing a number of junctions to which it is possible to connect the network cables coming from the computers. Its role is to ensure communication between the various junctions. This topology can be illustrated as in the figure below.

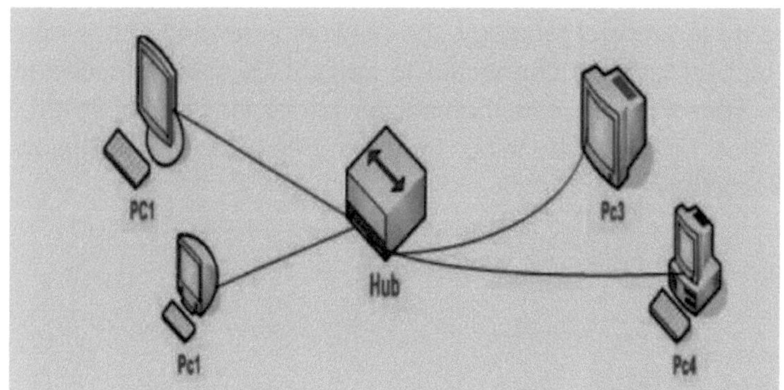

Unlike networks built on a bus topology, networks based on a star topology are much less vulnerable because one of the connections can be disconnected without paralysing the rest of the network. The nerve centre of this network is the central distribution frame, because without it, communication between the computers on the network is no longer possible. That's why we recommend special maintenance for the central distribution frame.

Note also that if the dispatcher is a hub, the information sent by the computers on the network is visible to all the machines on the network. If it is a switch that acts as the dispatcher, the information sent is sent directly to the recipient (knowing the source and destination addresses).

C. RING TOPOLOGY

In this topology, the computers are located on a loop (theoretically) and each communicate in turn. In reality, the computers are not connected in a loop, but are connected to a dispatcher (called MAU, Multi Station Access Unit) which will manage communication between the computers connected to it by allocating a talk time (token) to each of them. Token ring and FDDI are examples of networks using this topology.

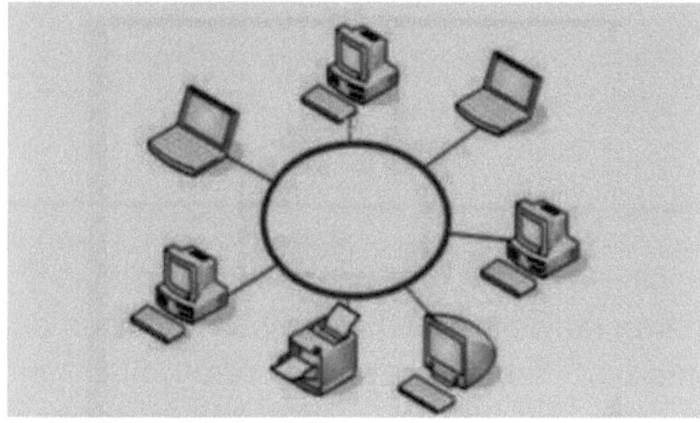

D. TREE TOPOLOGY

Also known as a hierarchical topology, the network is divided into levels. The top, the highest level, is connected to several lower-level nodes in the hierarchy. These nodes can themselves be connected to several lower-level nodes. The whole thing forms a tree. The figure below illustrates this topology.

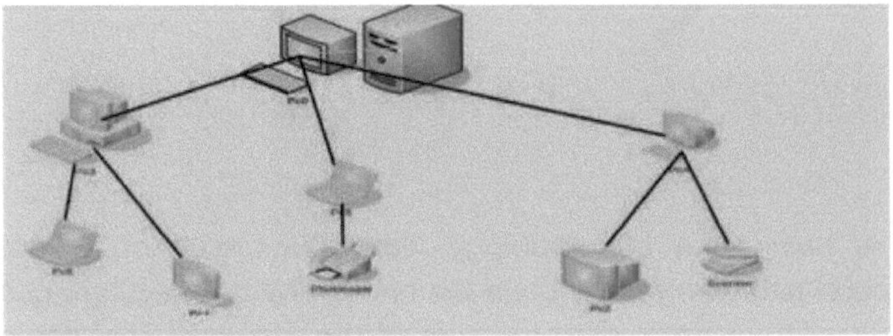

E. MESH TOPOLOGY

A mesh topology, an evolution of the star topology, corresponds to several point-to-point connections. A network unit can have (1, N) point-to-point connections to several other units. Each terminal is connected to all the others. The disadvantage is that the number of links required becomes very high. This topology is found in large distribution networks (e.g. the Internet). Information can travel through the network along various routes, under the control of powerful network supervisors, or using distributed routing methods. The figure below illustrates this topology.

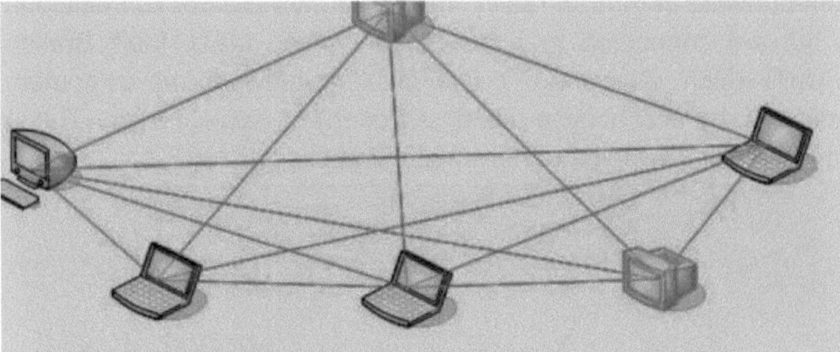

II. LOGICAL TOPOLOGY

> **Ethernet**: refers to a local area network (LAN) protocol. It is based on packet switching and twisted-pair cables to link several machines together. For private users, Ethernet is simply a cable connected between a computer and an Internet access point, providing high quality

data transfer.

> **Token Ring**: often used in ring topology where each computer is connected to the ring by two circuits: one for remission and the other for reception. The operating mode is identical to that of the ring topology.

FDDI: Fiber Distributed Data Interface, defines a high-performance network capable of carrying high-speed data with integrated administration.

CHAPTER II

WIRED NETWORKS

11.1. DEFINITIONS OF CONCEPTS

11.1.1. WIRE NETWORK

A wired network is a network in which equipment is linked and communicates via a wired connection (cable).

11.1.2. SERVER

A computer server is a device that offers a range of services to clients to which it is connected via a network over the Internet or an intranet.

11.1.3. IP ADDRESS

An IP address (Internet Protocol address) is a **series of numbers assigned to each device connected to a computer network or the Internet**.

IP addresses also make it possible to identify and differentiate between billions of online devices, including computers and mobile phones, and help them communicate with each other.

Other devices connected to the Internet, including printers and a growing number of connected objects such as smart speakers and fridges, home surveillance systems and more, also have an IP address.

IP ADDRESS DETAILS

An IP address generally consists of four numbers between 0 and 255, separated by dots. Each IP address comprises the **network ID**, assigned to your network by your ISP (Internet Service Provider), and the **host ID**, the unique identifier assigned to each device connected to that specific network.

Here is an example of an IP address:

172.16.254.1

Each of the four numbers in an IP address can be 1 to 3 digits long. In our example, the first number is 172, the second 16, the third 254 and the fourth 1. This set of decimal numbers separated by dots is called a 32-bit number.

The IP address is a series of numbers and dots that works like a postal address so that your device can send and receive data on the Internet.

11.1.4. ROUTER

A **router** is a piece of computer network interconnection equipment used to route packets between two or more networks in order to determine the path that a data packet will take.

II.1.5.CUSTOMER COMPUTER

The client computer is generally an ordinary personal computer, acting in this context as a terminal: it is equipped with software relating to the different types of requests that will be sent.

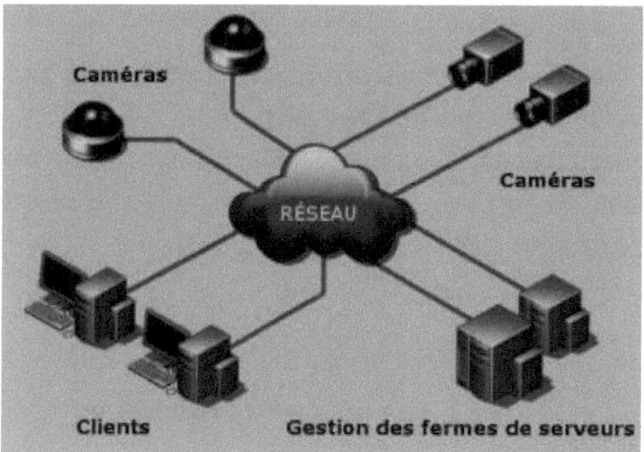

11.2. EQUIPMENT FOR INSTALLING A WIRED NETWORK

To set up a wired network you'll need a hub, switch or router that connects to the various devices on the network via cables. You will need to fit all the devices with an Ethernet network adapter to ensure that the Ethernet connection is compatible. Most computers have built-in Ethernet network adapters.

A. HUB

B. SWITCH (ROUTER)

C. ETHERNET CABLE

Ethernet cable definition: This is a cable used for transmitting **computer**

data. It is used to connect your console, your TV decoder or your computer to an Internet connection. It links your livebox to the device you want to connect.

Ethernet cable also goes by the nickname "**wired connection**", because unlike Wi-Fi, which lets you connect to the Internet without using a cable, Ethernet cable is, as its name suggests, the cable that connects you to a connection. There are a multitude of them, each with its own structural differences. This is why they are also classified into categories.

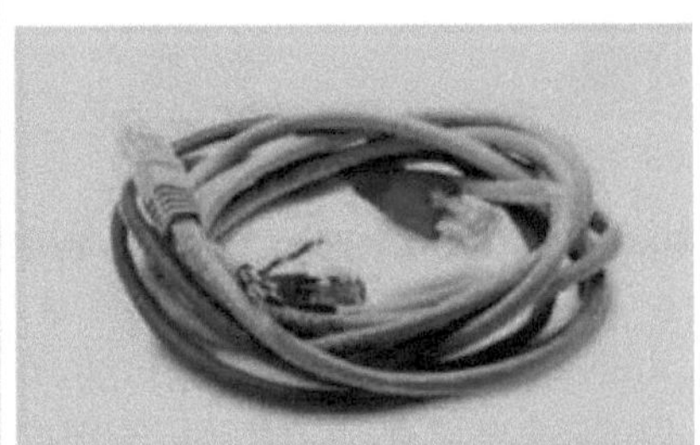

D. COMPUTER

11.3. CONFIGURING A WIRED NETWORK

To configure a wired network, please follow the steps below.

Connect an **Ethernet cable** to the modem/router in the port labelled "LAN" or "Ethernet". Connect the other end to your computer. In Windows, go to **Start "Settings**

"Network and Internet "Ethernet check "Connected".

CHAPTER III

WIRELESS NETWORK

A wireless network refers to a computer network that uses radio frequency (RF) connections between network nodes.

3.1. 1.DEFINITIONS OF BASIC CONCEPTS

3.1.1.1. MODEM

A modem is a box used to establish a connection to the Internet. After entering a user name and password, the modem connects to your Internet Service Provider (ISP) to authenticate itself and allow you to surf the Internet. Boxes like the Freebox and Livebox are both a modem and a router.

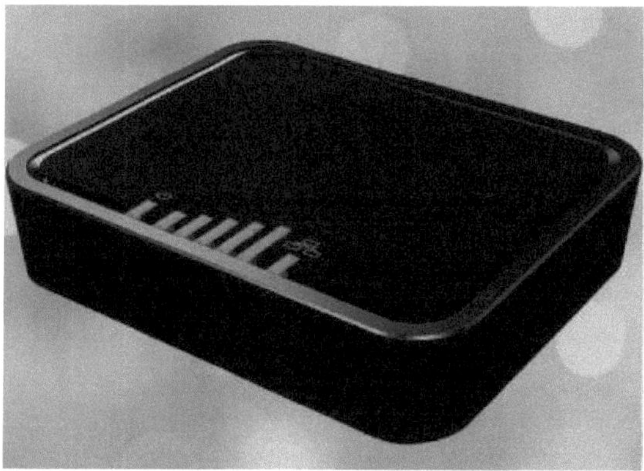

3.1.2.2.NETWORK MAP

The network card is **the interface between your computer and the network.**

3.1.3.3. WIRELESS NETWORK CARD

A wireless network card is a **device that connects your PC to a wireless network.**

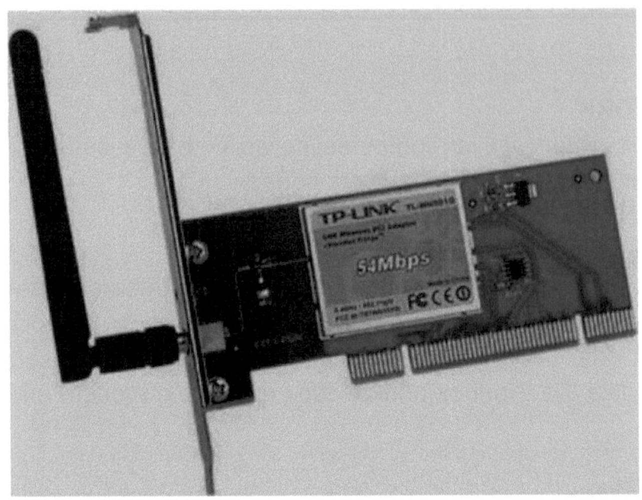

3.1.4.4.WIFI

Wi-Fi, which stands for "Wireless Fidelity", is a wireless networking technology that allows electronic devices to connect seamlessly to a network via radio frequencies.

3.1.5.5.ACCESS POINT

An access point (AP) is a network device that links a wired network to a wireless network.

Most access points connect to wireless networks using the Wi-Fi standard. However, modern commercial and industrial access points increasingly support the Bluetooth and Thread wireless standards, enabling them to support both user devices and IoT (Internet of Things) equipment.

3.2. 2.WIRELESS NETWORK TYPES AND TECHNOLOGIES

A wireless network is, as its name suggests, a network in which at least two devices can communicate without a wired link. Wireless networks use radio waves (radio and infrared) instead of the usual cables. There are a number of technologies, which differ in terms of the transmission frequency used, as well as the speed and range of transmissions.

Wireless networks are usually divided into several categories, depending on the geographical area offering connectivity (coverage zone), as follows:

A. WWAN (Wireless Wide Area Network),

The extended wireless network: Also known as the mobile cellular network. This is the most widespread wireless network, since all mobile phones are connected to an extended wireless network. The main technologies are GSM (Global System for Mobile communication), GPRS (General Packet Radio Service) and UMTS (Universal Mobile Telecommunications System).

B. WMAN (Wireless Metropolitan Area Network),

The wireless metropolitan area network Known as the radio local loop (RLL). WMANs are based on the IEEE 802.16 standard. The best-known metropolitan wireless network standard is WiMAX, which delivers speeds of around 70 Mbps over a radius of several kilometres.

C. WLAN (Wireless Area Network), wireless local area network

A network covering the equivalent of a company local area network, i.e. a range of around one hundred metres. It enables terminals within the coverage area to be linked together.

There are several competing technologies: wifi or IEEE 802.11 and HiperLAN2 (High performance Radio LAN 2.0).

D. WPAN (Wireless Personal Area Network), wireless personal area network

Also known as individual wireless networks or home wireless networks, these are wireless networks with a short range, of the order of a few dozen metres. This type of network uses Bluetooth, HomeRF (Home Radio Frequency), Zigbee (also known as IEEE 802.15.4) and infrared technologies.

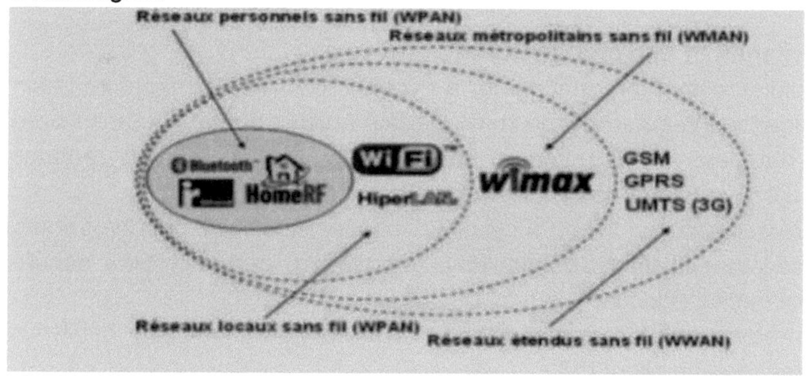

CHAPTER IV

CLIENT-SERVER SYSTEMS

IV.1.DEFINITIONS OF CONCEPTS

IV.1.1. POINT-TO-POINT MODE

A **point-to-point link** is a link between two hosts only and is not designed to be used initially in a network. There is therefore no native notion of the network address of the two hosts, and no advance control of the flow.

IV.1.2.CLIENT-SERVER

Client-server generally refers to two processes, one of which is the client and the other the server. This architecture is based on a central station, the server, which sends data to the client machines. Programs that access the server are called client programs (FTP client, mail client, etc.).

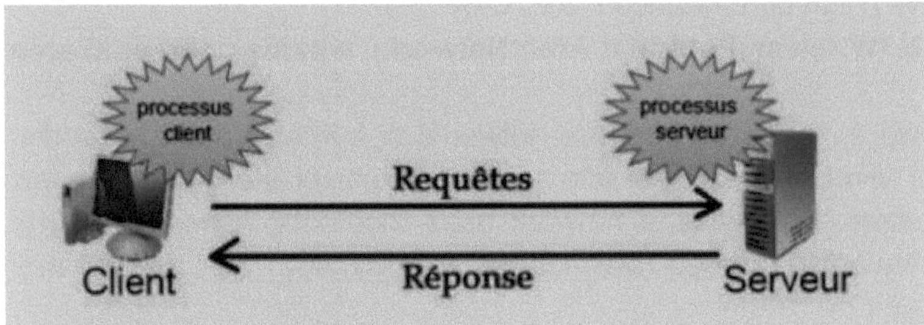

Advantages of this architecture :

> Uniqueness of information: for a dynamic website, for example (such as vulgarisation-informatique.com), certain articles on the site are stored in a database on the server. In this way, the information remains identical. Every user has access to the same information.

> Greater security: When a client PC connects, it only sees the server, not the other client PCs. Similarly, servers are generally very secure against hacker attacks.

> Greater reliability: In the event of a breakdown, only the server is repaired, not the client PC.

> Scalability: A client/server architecture is scalable because it's very easy to add or remove clients, and even servers.

Disadvantages of this architecture

> High operating costs (bandwidth, cables, powerful computers)

IV.1.3.DATA SERVER

Database servers bring together all your data, whether from mission-critical software or email clients, creating a 'one-stop shop' for your data and information storage and management needs. Ideal if you need to access information on a regular basis, or to better manage your databases using a reliable network system.

IV.1.4. PRINT SERVER

Whether it's to print employment contracts for the HR department, order forms for the sales department or flyers for the marketing teams, every company has printers. And often several, so that they can be distributed between the different departments. So to manage all the documents to be printed, organisations need a print server. We take a closer look at this technology, which is essential for every business.

What is a print server?

The print server is a **network device that connects the company's printers and computers.** This means that several employees can use the same printer.

Acting as an intermediary, this server must **manage print requests** between computers and printers. In practical terms, when an employee wants to print a document, they send a request via their computer to the print server. The print server will then send the request to the right printer in order to fulfil the employee's print request.

By managing all a company's printing, this equipment is more than essential to its smooth running, both for internal processes and for relations with third parties.

PRINT SERVER FUNCTIONS

The print server's main role is to manage all print requests from all computers on the IT network. As such, it must :

- **Connect computers and printers**: the print server shares one or more printers with the organisation's computers, so that all employees can use them.
- **Send requests to the right printer**: a company often has several printers. The server needs to send the right print request (colour, black and white, number of pages, etc.) to the right place.
- **Manage simultaneous print requests**: if the printer is already busy, the server stores and queues the request. This avoids overloading the printing device.

. **Centralising requests**: for companies working in large buildings (especially when are several floors), the print server is more than essential as it centralises requests from all the computers in the structure.

- **Organise the queue**: as well as printing all types of document, you can reorganise the queue, prioritise jobs and delete queued documents from the print server.

Thanks to all these features, businesses save a considerable amount of time when printing documents. Whatever your needs. In fact, it is always possible to add other client systems or printers to the IT network. The print server will continue to centralise all requests.

PRINT SERVER LIMITS

While the print server is essential for managing all the organisation's print requests simultaneously, it does have one major drawback. If it suffers a bug or breakdown, all the printers connected to the peripheral are affected. In other words, the company can no longer print anything until the problem is resolved. And this can have a major impact on the productivity of its teams. This is particularly true for companies with very high printing requirements or that have not yet completed their digital transformation.

NB: the print server is integrated with all the other technological resources of an organisation. Administrators must therefore take them into account when managing the IT system and do their utmost to limit any breakdowns or bugs that could paralyse the company's printing.

PRINT SERVER OPERATION

To operate, a print server needs :

. A network input to manage network protocols. This is often an RJ45 port for the Ethernet network.

- One or more outputs to connect each to the printers. This can be a parallel, USB or wireless connection (although most print servers have USB output connections).

NB: the print server can take the form of a host computer with several shared printers or a separate device implementing the print protocols. Whichever it is, the functionalities remain the same.

CONFIGURING A PRINT SERVER

Print server configuration depends on the operating system used. As most companies use Windows, we are concentrating on this system. Windows Servers are installed by default for Microsoft and TCP/IP networks. The operations to be carried out then depend on the server version. But in general, you should click on "Configure Server Wizard", then "Print Server" and go to the "Printers and Printer Drivers" page. You can then add or remove a local printer.

IV.1.5.MAIL SERVER

A mail server (sometimes called an email server) is software that sends and reports emails.

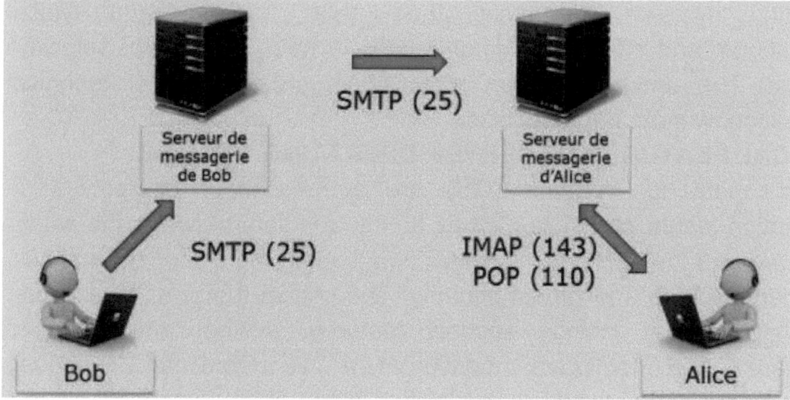

IV.1.6.APPLICATION SERVER

Application servers are defined as a server that enables applications to be installed, operated and hosted. While residing on the server side, it provides the business logic behind the application. The three elements of a functional Web programme are the operating system, external resources such as the database management system (DBMS), Internet services and the user's application. Application servers sit between these three elements.

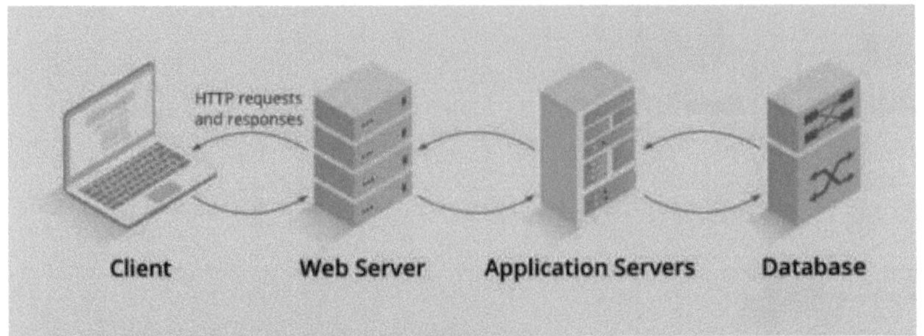

IV.2. OPERATING SYSTEMS USED

Choosing the right server operating system in 2024 requires an in-depth understanding of the different systems and their respective capabilities. This article provides an informative comparison of the main server operating systems, discusses their main features and typical applications, and offers recommendations to help you in your selection process. The emphasis is on professional presentation of technical information, without personal bias.

CRITICAL FEATURES OF SERVER OPERATING SYSTEMS

Server operating systems (OS) are an essential component in information technology. They act as an intermediary between the server hardware and the applications running on it, ensuring smooth operations, high performance and robust security. The critical functions of a server operating system include security features, system administration, hardware and software configuration requirements, workload management and networking capabilities. Each of these aspects plays a key role in the overall performance and efficiency of a server.

SERVER OPERATING SYSTEM SECURITY FEATURES

Security is of paramount importance in server operating systems. A secure server operating system offers robust protection against unauthorised access, data breaches and other cyber threats. It should include features such as firewall settings, user authentication and authorisation mechanisms, intrusion detection systems and encryption tools. In addition, it must also have regular updates and patches to address any emerging security vulnerabilities.

SYSTEM ADMINISTRATION IN SERVER OPERATING SYSTEMS

System administration in server operating systems involves the management and maintenance of the server's operating environment. This includes tasks such as installing and configuring the server, installing and updating software applications, monitoring system performance, performing regular backups and troubleshooting any problems that may arise. A good server operating system will provide efficient, user-friendly tools for system administration, making these tasks more accessible and manageable.

HARDWARE AND SOFTWARE REQUIREMENTS FOR SERVER OPERATING SYSTEMS

The hardware and software requirements of a server operating system depend on the specific needs of the organisation and the applications that will run on the server. Typically, the server operating system requires a powerful processor, sufficient memory and sufficient storage capacity. On the software side, the server operating system must support the necessary applications and services required by the organisation. It must also be compatible with the server hardware to ensure optimum performance.

BEST PRACTICE IN WORKLOAD MANAGEMENT

WORKING IN SERVER OPERATING SYSTEMS

Effective workload management in server operating systems is crucial to maintaining high performance and avoiding system overloads. This involves balancing the distribution of tasks across server resources, monitoring system usage to detect any potential bottlenecks and implementing strategies to optimise resource utilisation. Some server operating systems also offer advanced workload management features, such as load balancing and automatic resource allocation.

SERVER OPERATING SYSTEM NETWORKING CAPABILITIES

The network capabilities of a server operating system determine the extent to which it can communicate with other systems and devices on the network. This includes features such as network protocol support, bandwidth management and network security options. A server operating system with strong networking capabilities can facilitate seamless data transfer, efficient remote access and secure network connections, all of which are crucial to the smooth running of an organisation's IT infrastructure.

CHOOSING THE BEST SERVER OPERATING SYSTEM

Selecting the best server operating system (OS) is a crucial decision that can have a significant impact on the effectiveness and efficiency of your IT infrastructure. It involves understanding the different types of server operating systems, assessing the specific needs of your business, comparing the features and capabilities of different server operating systems, taking security aspects into account and evaluating integration with existing hardware and software. Let's look at each of these aspects in more detail.

IV.3.DIFFERENCE BETWEEN A POINT-TO-POINT SYSTEM AND A CLIENT-SERVER SYSTEM

We've been working with computers for a long time, so you may have heard the terms Client-server and Peer-to-Peer. These two network models are common ones that we use in our everyday lives. Client-Server architecture focuses on information sharing, while Peer-to-Peer architecture focuses on connectivity to remote computers.

The main difference between the Client-Server and Peer-to-Peer network models is that in the Client-Server model, data management is centralised, whereas in Peer-to-Peer, each user has their own data and applications. In addition, we will discuss more of the differences between Client-server and Peer-to-Peer architecture using the comparison table below.

COMPARISON TABLE

	CLIENT-SERVER	**PEER-TO-PEER**
Definition	There is a specific server and specific clients connected to the server.	The client and server do the same work. Each nreud acts as client and server.
Service	The client requests the service and the server offers the service.	Each node can request services and can also provide services.
Stability	The client-server model is more stable and scalable.	Peer-to-peer suffers if the number of peers in the system increases.
The cost	Client-server is expensive to implement	Peer-to-peer is cheaper to implement.
Rating Server	When several clients request services at the same time, one server can become overloaded.	As the services are provided by several servers distributed throughout the peer-to-peer system, one server is not overcrowded.
The data	The data is stored on a central server.	Each peer has its own data.

IV.4.BENEFITS

The main advantages of the client-server network are security, reliability and scalability. The central server makes it possible to access data remotely and save it on a secure server. It also offers greater scalability, as thousands of users can be connected without affecting network speed or performance.

IV.5.LIMITS OF TWO SYSTEMS

1. Client-server technology does have a few limitations, however:

- **High cost:** Servers can be expensive to set up and maintain.
- **In the event of a breakdown:** a failure of the central server could disrupt all the computers or other devices on the client-server network.
- **Traffic congestion:** When a large number of clients send requests to the same server, the server may not be able to cope with the load, which can lead to traffic congestion .

2. The main drawback of peer-to-peer networks is that they are highly susceptible to viruses and malware. When you download files on a P2P network, you can never be sure of the quality of the files you are downloading.

What's more, because users are connected directly to each other, there is no data filtering. This can make the network vulnerable to computer attacks and content piracy. **NB:** Both client-server and peer-to-peer networks have their own advantages and limitations. And both models can give good performance if used in appropriate environments. You'll need to weigh up the advantages and disadvantages of each network model to decide which one to implement.

IV.6. DNS SERVER

The Domain Name System (DNS) is the service that provides the link between the domain name and the IP address of a server. It means that Internet users do not need to know the exact IP address of a website in order to access it.

IV.6.1.OPERATING A DNS SERVER

When a domain name is entered in a browser, the request is sent to the DNS server. The DNS server responds by providing the IP address of the associated web server. The browser can then send its request to the target server, and send the Internet user back the requested data, i.e. the website they are looking for. At OVHcloud, your DNS server is included at no extra cost and can be used with your domain name, web hosting, CDN, SSL and e-mail accounts.

IV.6.2.FROM DNS REQUEST TO WEB PAGE DISPLAY

A web search triggers a series of steps enabling the user to access the content they want to consult.

1. Via their Internet connection, Internet users enter a URL, "ovhcloud.com" for example, into a browser. This request is sent by the

modem-router to the DNS resolver, which is responsible for resolving the domain name.

2. The DNS resolver, usually that of the Internet Service Provider (ISP), reports the request and forwards it to the DNS root server.
3. The root server responds by indicating the server corresponding to the TLD (Top-level domain) extension associated with the domain being searched for, in this case .com.
4. The DNS resolver sends the request to the .com name server. It then responds by indicating the DNS server in charge of the domain name being searched for.
5. The ISP's resolver sends the request to the DNS server, which looks up the IP addresses and provides the one corresponding to the web server associated with the "ovhcloud.com" domain name.
6. The IP address is transmitted to the browser and stored in a DNS cache for faster subsequent consultation.
7. The web browser submits the HTTP (Hypertext Transfer Protocol) request ovhcloud.com to the web server corresponding to the IP given by the DNS resolver.
8. The web server responds by returning the content corresponding to ovhcloud.com, i.e. the home page of our website.

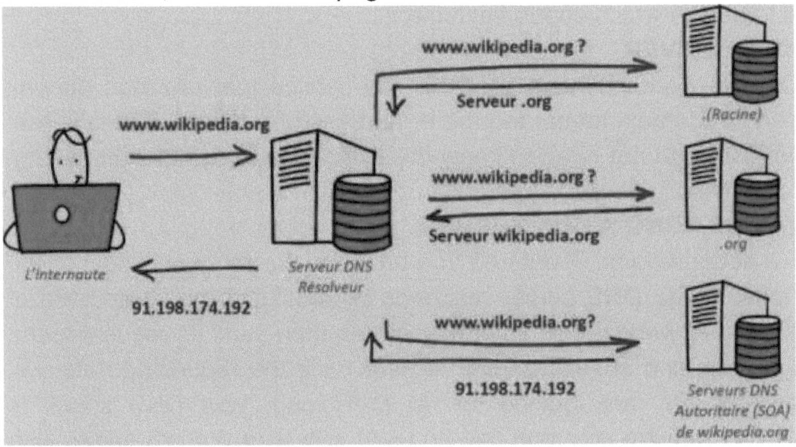

IV.7.DHCP

A DHCP server, or DHCP service, allocates IP addresses to devices connected to the network. In general, the network cards of these devices are waiting for an IP address so that they can communicate on the network. In addition to the IP address, the DHCP service also provides additional information about the network to which the device is connected.

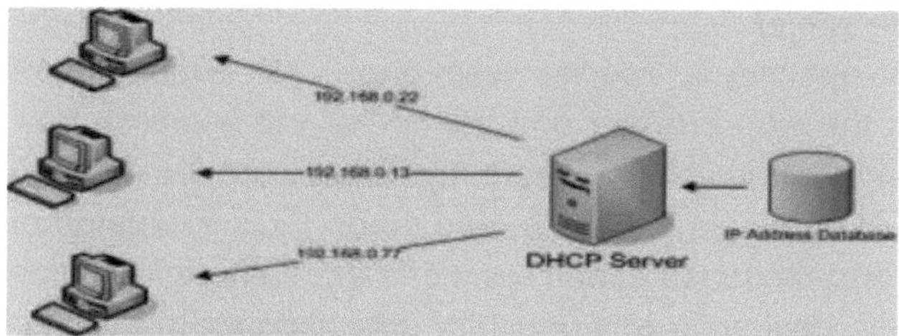

IV.8.http PROTOCOLS

Hypertext Transfer Protocol (HTTP) is the **communications protocol** used to transfer information via files (HTML) on the World Wide Web. Conceived in the early 1990s, HTTP is an extensible protocol that has evolved over time. It is what is known as an application layer protocol protocol, and is transmitted using TCP or TLS. Because it is extensible, it is used not only to transmit HTTP hypertext documents, but also images or videos, or to send data or content to servers, as in the case of forms.
The HTTP method is the basis of all data exchange on the Web. It follows a **request-response schema** between a client and a server. Each user action, such as entering a URL or clicking on a link, is converted into an HTTP request to the server. The server then sends a response message back to the client, so that the user sees the result of the request displayed in the browser.
The HTTP protocol operates on top of the TCP/IP protocol suite, which forms the basis of the Internet. The latest version of HTTP is HTTP/2, which was released in May 2015.
HTTP is also a stateless protocol, meaning that it does not store any information about previous connections. Web applications often need to maintain state. To do this, we use cookies, which are pieces of information that a server can store on the client's system. This allows Web applications to track users and their online activity, as cookies can be stored on the client for an indefinite period of time.

IV.8.1.HTTP OPERATION

HTTP works on a "request-response" basis between the web server and the user agent, in other words, the client requesting data transmission. A client can be a web browser or the web *crawlers* or *web spiders* that inspect existing pages.
The server provides the client with a structured response with a series of metadata, which establishes the directives for launching, developing and closing the transmission of information. These are the **request methods**,

i.e. the commands that trigger the execution of specific resources whose files are stored on the server.

For example, when opening a specific web page, the exchange of information between the web browser and the server will establish how the information should be transmitted, where the images are located and in what order they will be displayed to me, and so on. This exchange of request commands and response codes results in the same information being displayed on the device as was originally contained on the server, which may be thousands of miles away.

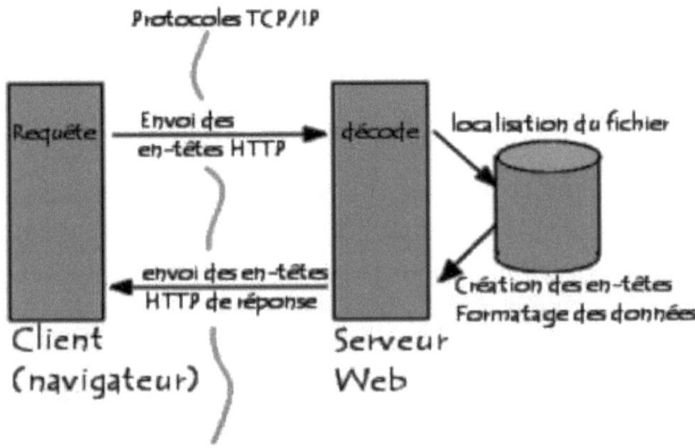

IV.9.SMTP PROTOCOL

Simple Mail Transfer Protocol (SMTP) is the technology that **governs the entire process of sending emails**.

Introduced in 1982, the SMTP protocol has become the global standard for email transmission. In short, SMTP is a set of rules that mail servers follow to ensure that emails are delivered from the sending server to the receiving server.

With TurboSMTP, you can maximise the use of these regimes, guaranteeing not only the delivery of your emails, but also a higher open rate by avoiding spam filters.

IV.9.1.OPERATION OF SMTP PROTOCOL: FROM SENDING TO DELIVERY

The SMTP protocol facilitates communication between email clients (such as Gmail or Outlook) and mail servers on the Internet.

In short, when you send an email, **your email client connects to an SMTP server** to start the message delivery process.

How exactly does SMTP work?

- **Sender authentication:** the SMTP server first checks the sender's identity using commands such as HELO or EHLO. This step ensures that the email comes from a legitimate source, helping to prevent spam or malicious emails. With TurboSMTP, this process is optimised to minimise the risk of your emails becoming spam.

. **Recipient verification:** after authenticating the sender, the SMTP server verifies the recipient address with the RCPT TO command. This ensures that the email is sent to a valid address.

. **Message transmission:** after verification, the content of the email (subject, body, attachments) is transmitted to the recipient's server using the DATA command.

. **SMTP relay:** if the recipient's server is temporarily inaccessible, SMTP can relay the email via different servers until it reaches its final destination. This relay capability is

This is crucial for guaranteeing the delivery of emails on a global scale, preventing messages from being lost or blocked en route.

Thanks to a robust infrastructure, TurboSMTP has optimised this process, ensuring high availability and reliable deliveries, even in cases where additional relay servers are required to reach the final recipient.

- **Error handling:** in the event of a problem, the SMTP server can queue the email and try to send it later, or send an error back to the sender.

TurboSMTP optimises this process, offering advanced statistics and improved error management.

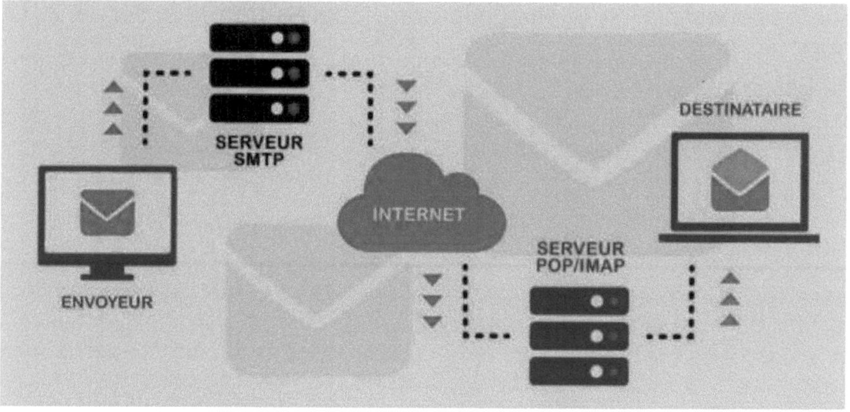

IV.10.POP3 PROTOCOL

Post Office Protocol 3 (POP3 for short) is a method of receiving email.

POP3 is a transmission protocol that allows an e-mail client to retrieve e-mail from a server.
POP3 is the right choice for you if you're concerned about time spent online for cost reasons. With this procedure, emails are always transmitted from the server to the local device.
If you only receive and read your emails on a specific computer, you can use POP3 without hesitation.

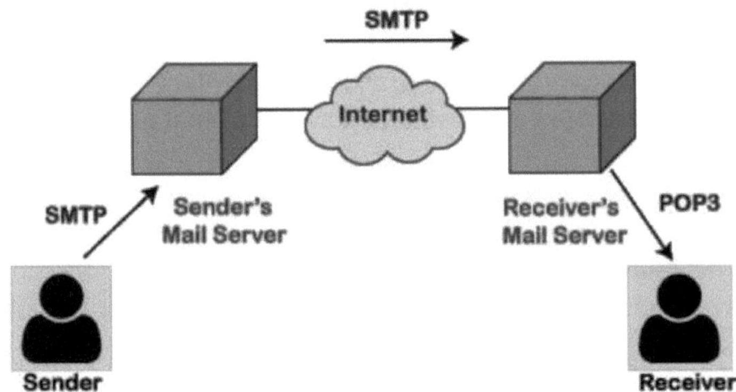

IV.11.INSTALLATION AND CONFIGURATION PROCESS FOR A SERVER

Using **Windows Server 2012 R2 Essentials** as an example, several steps are required to install and configure this system. The following tutorial (illustrated) guides you through the process.

IV.11.1.INSTALLATION

The basic installation is straightforward, booting from the Server 2012 DVD
R2 Essentials

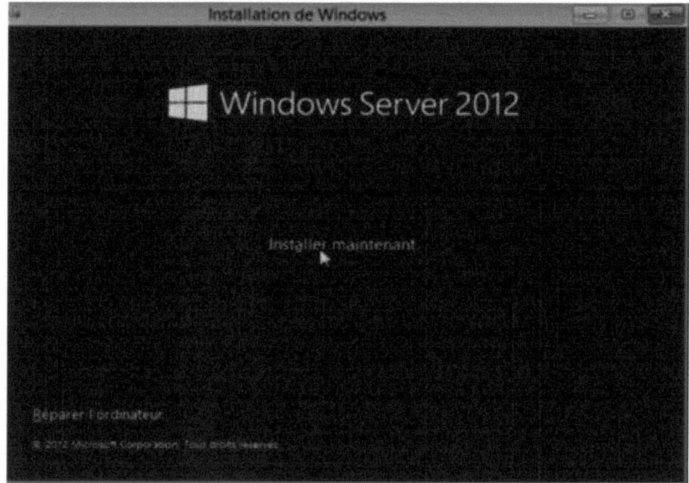

Then enter the Microsoft Windows server product key

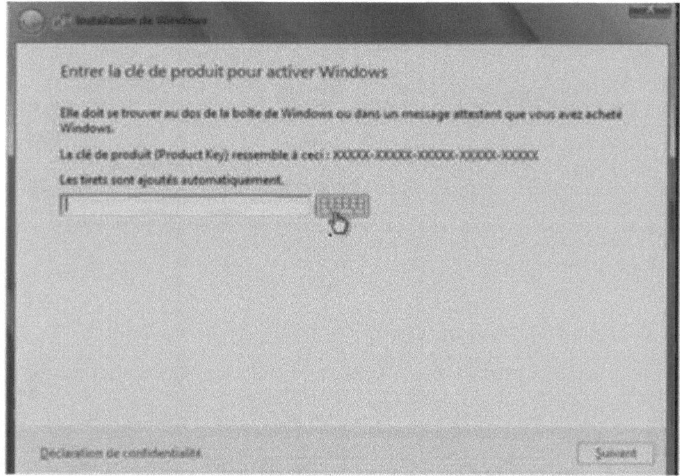

We accept the user contract

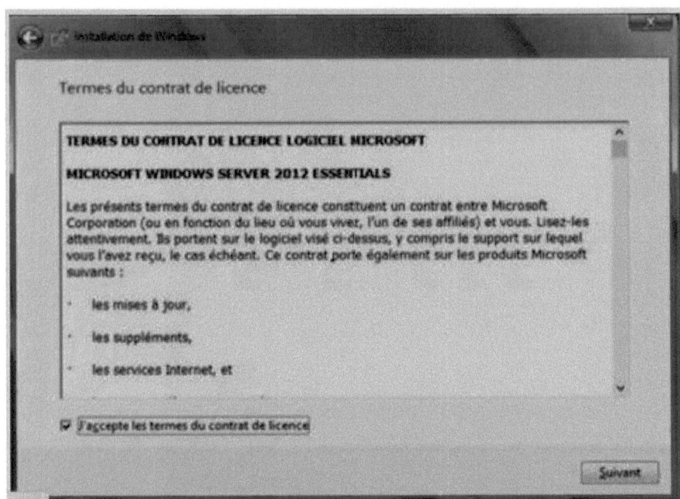

Choose Custom installation

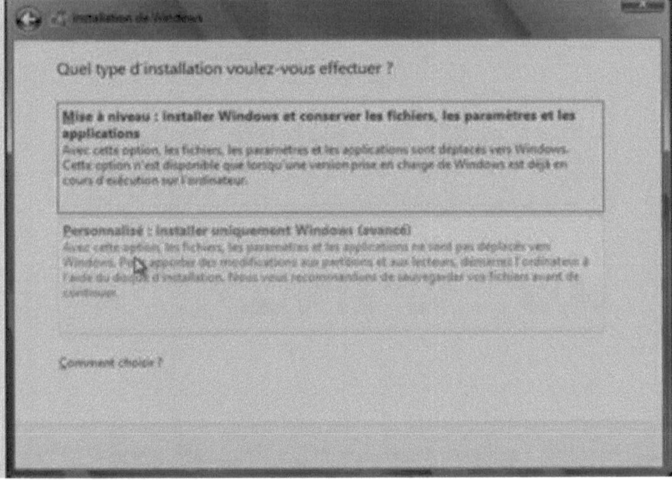

Choose the disk and accept automatic formatting and partitioning (you can define another partition)

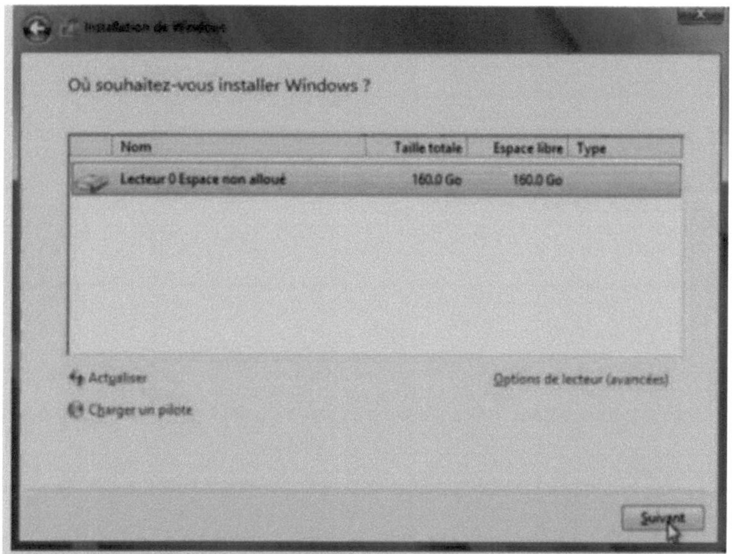

Starting the installation: the rest of the installation steps run automatically
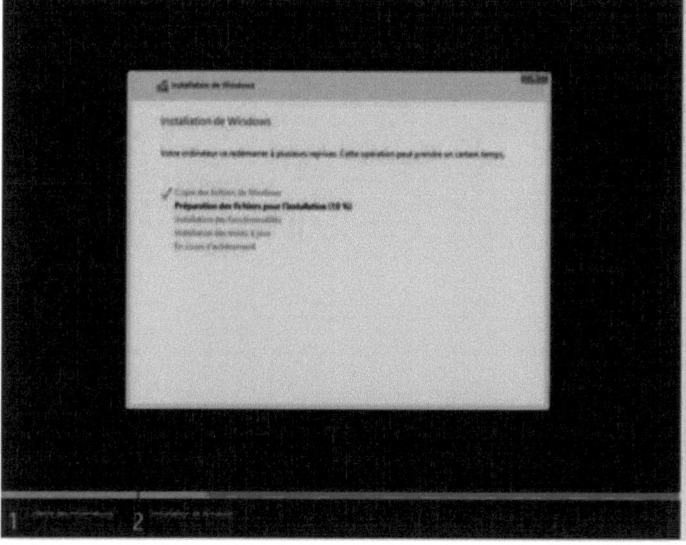

Setting the date and time

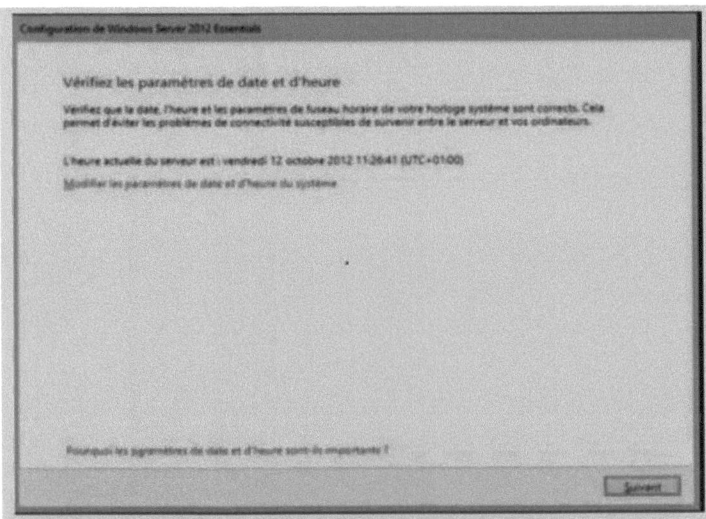

Enter the password for the administrator account

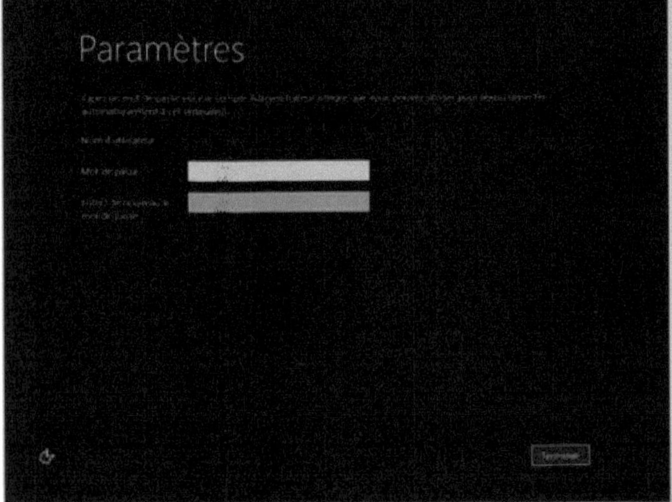

The installation is complete and the session opens with the administrator account

The installation is now complete and we're going to move on to the configuration stage, which involves two processes

FIRST PART OF THE CONFIGURATION

Here your installation program first performs basic verification tasks and creates your server according to your choice (company name, domain name, server name). Then start the configuration as follows:

The server starts by checking the system configuration.

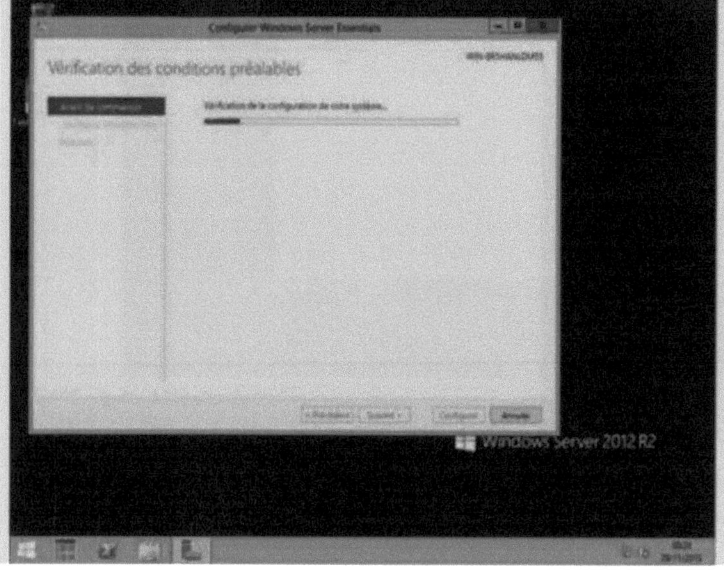

Once the verification is complete, it will start the configuration wizard for you to enter the basic settings.

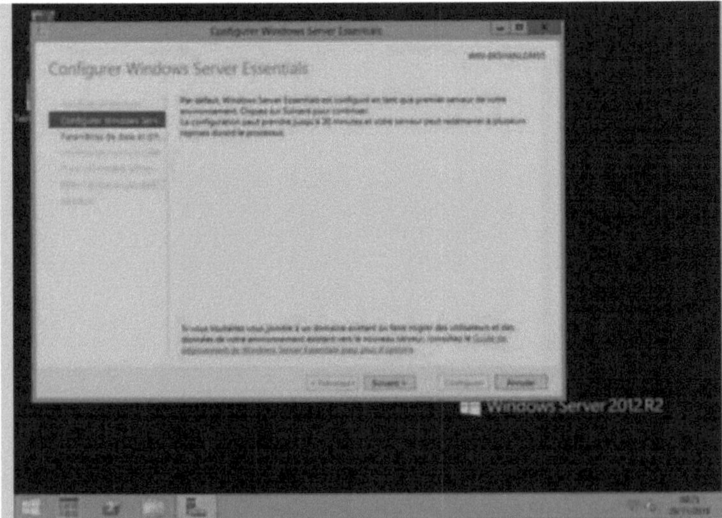

Then enter the time parameters.

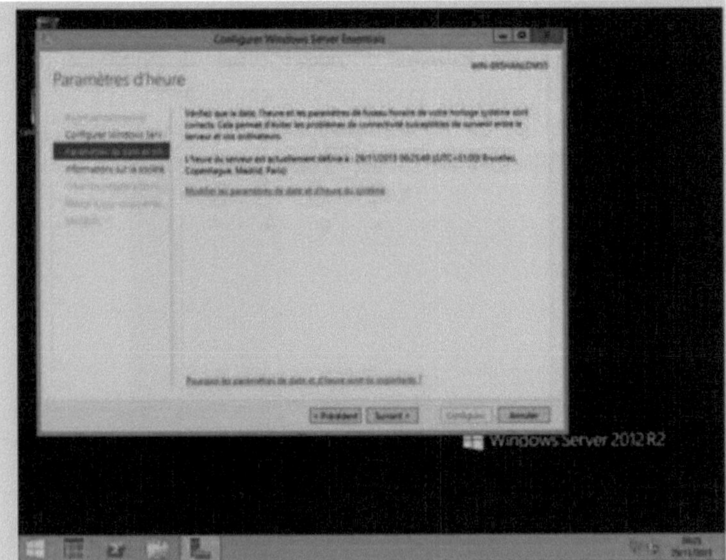

Enter your company name, internal Windows domain and server name.

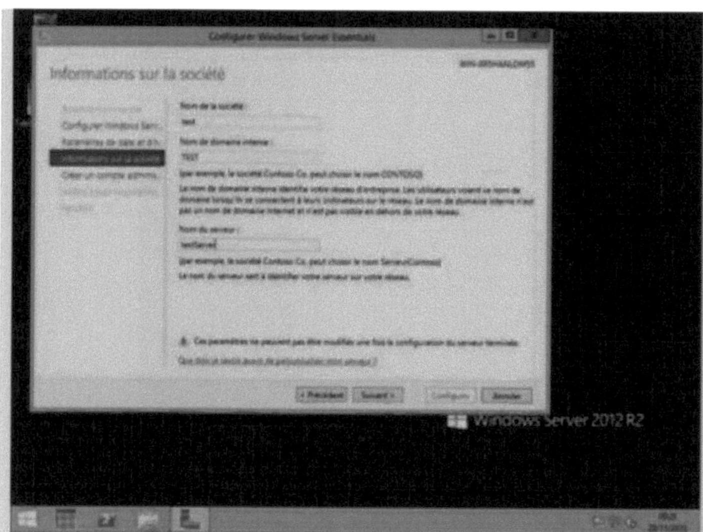

You then need to provide the administrator account and password.

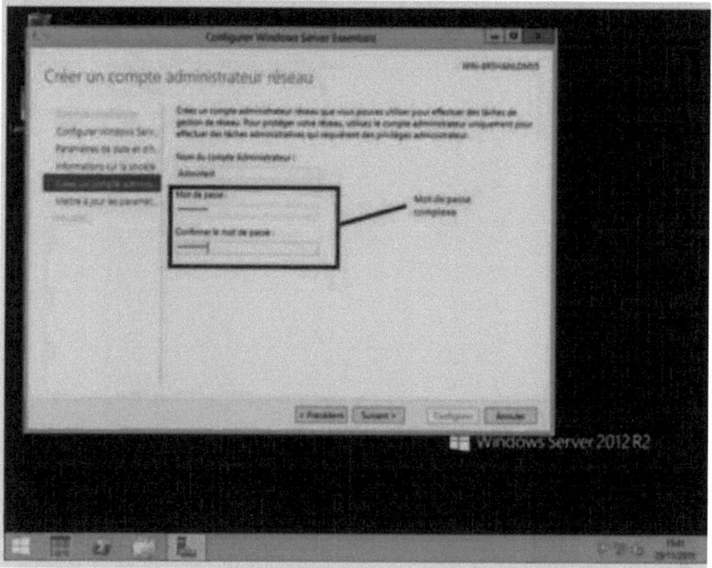

As far as the update option is concerned, it's best to use the recommended settings.

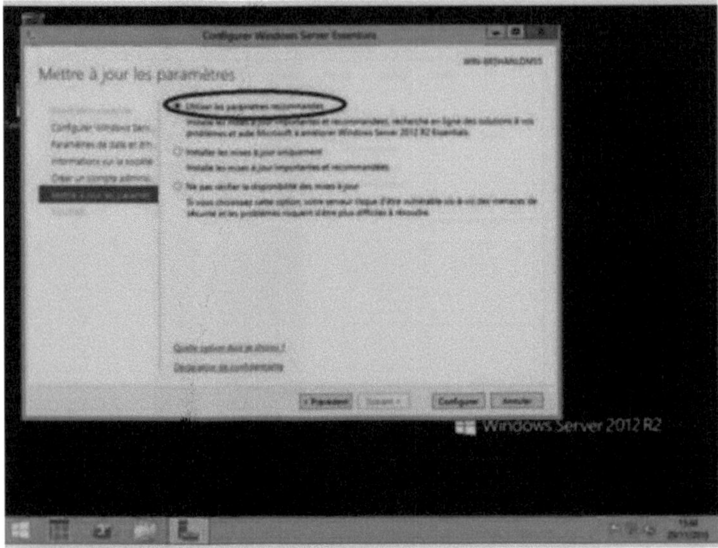

The configuration is now complete.

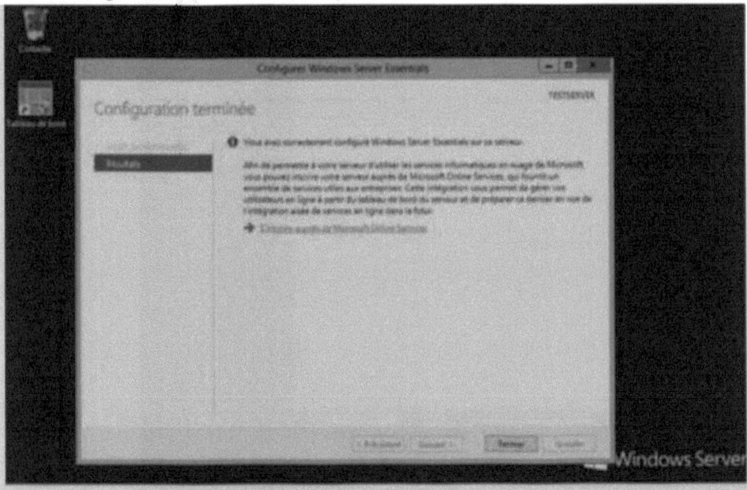

At this stage, five directories have been created. These are :

1. C:/Server Folders/Data redirection
2. C:/Server Folders/Backup file history
3. C:/Server Folders/Client Computer Backup
4. C:/Server Folders/Company
5. C:/Server Folders/users

It is recommended that you create a control point here to have a backed-up image of the system. In the case of a VM (Virtual Machine), you can use a snapshot.

SECOND PART OF THE CONFIGURATION

This is where the actual configuration of the Windows Essentials server takes place. And Microsoft has created a dashboard grouping together the various administration tasks:

- Create an account.
- Share a folder.

. Connect a PC.

. Configure server backup.

CREATING AN ACCOUNT

To create a user account, you need :

. Open the dashboard and select "add user accounts".

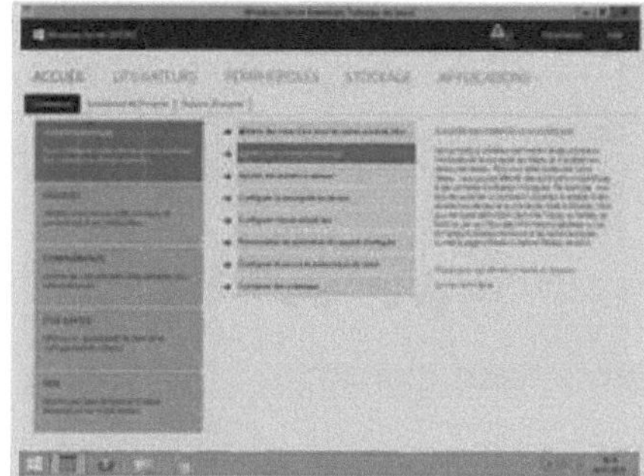

Enter user information.

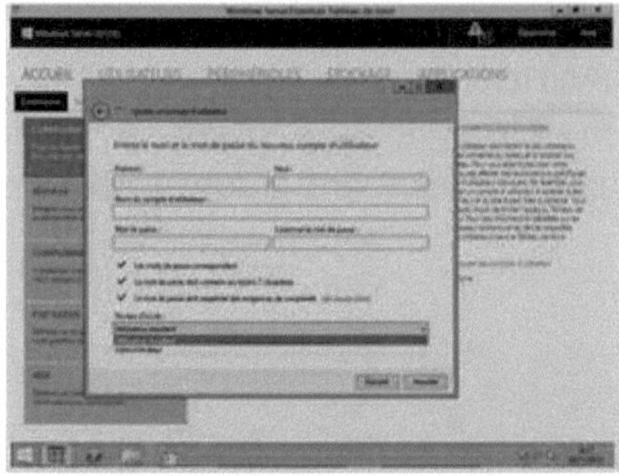

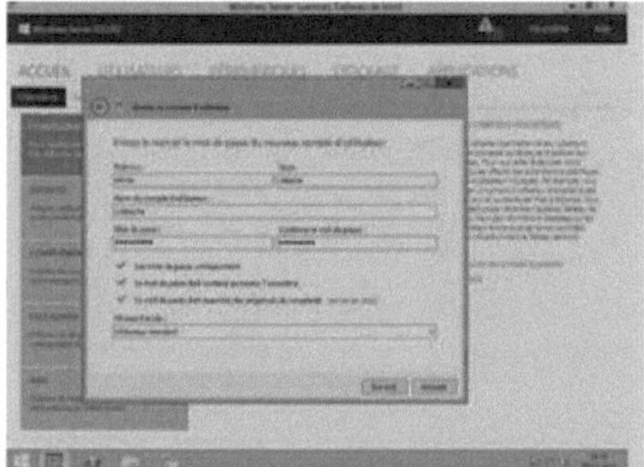

Select the access level on the company's basic directory.

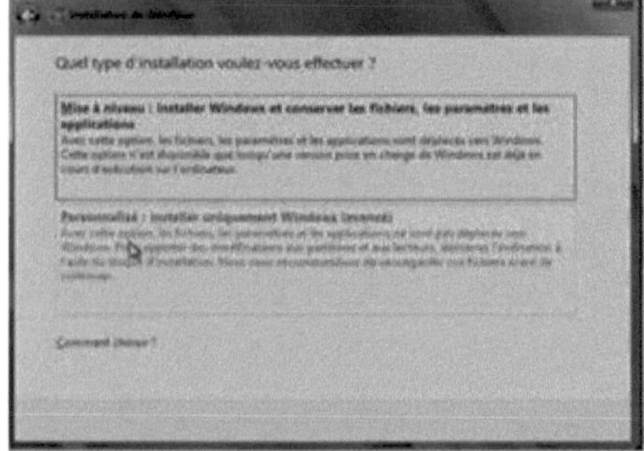

Enable network access to the server.

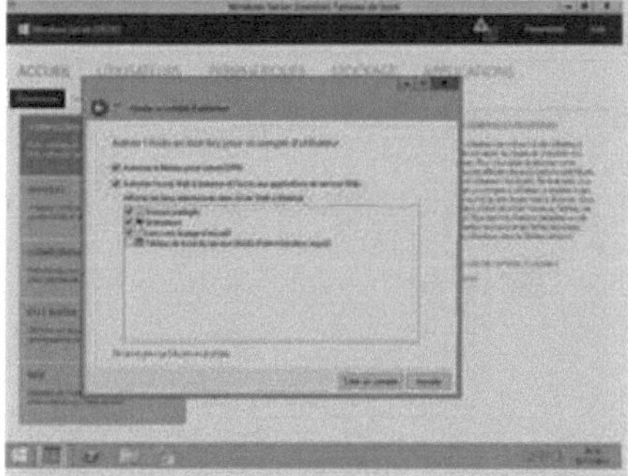

The account is now correctly configured.

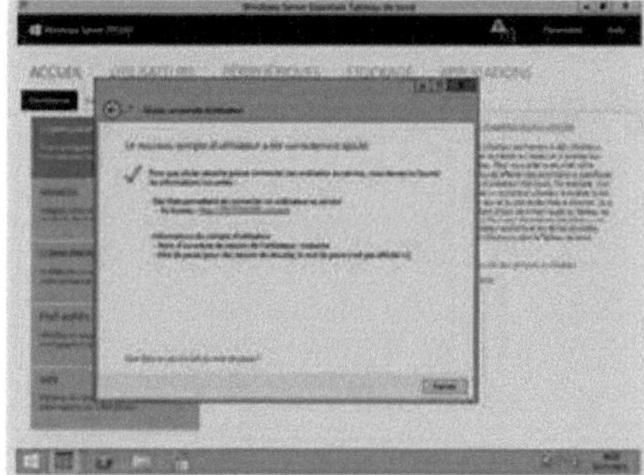

BACKING UP DATA

The idea is to go back to the dashboard and :

Start the backup configuration by clicking on the button is shown below.

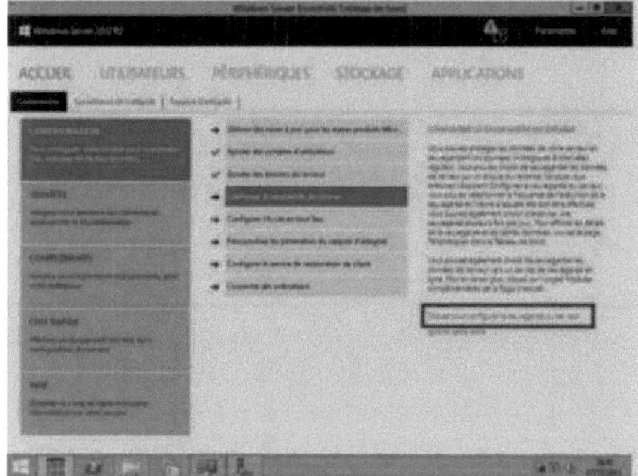

The configuration wizard loads.

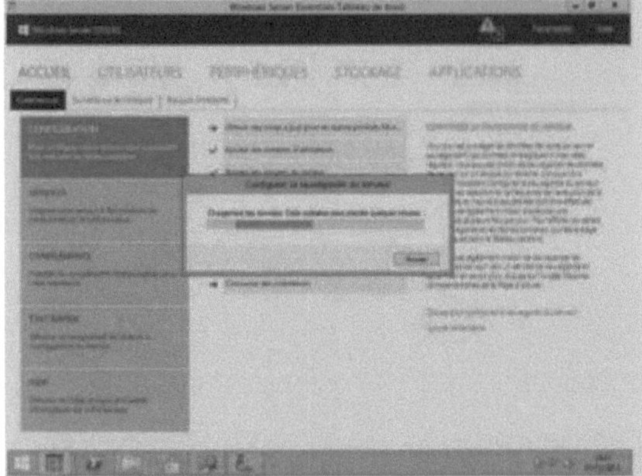

A summary of the actions to be defined is displayed.

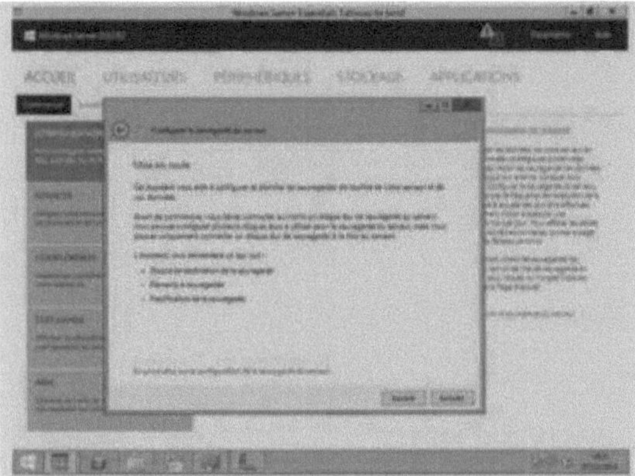

Choose the backup destination: Qa can be an external disk connected to the server.

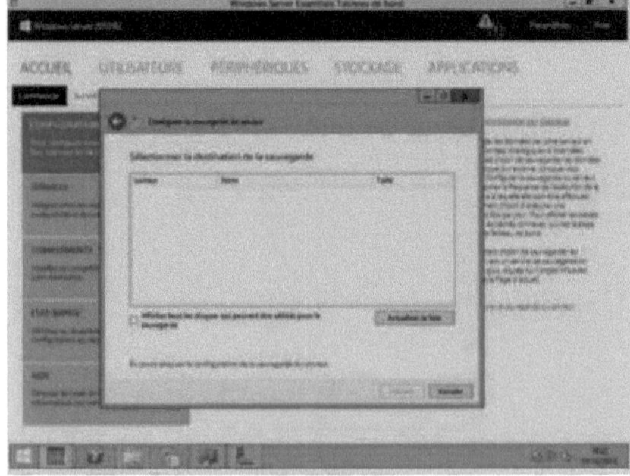

The disk will be partitioned

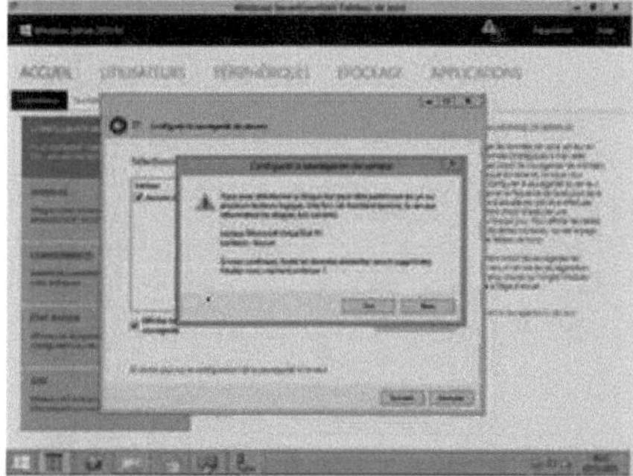

Give the disc a name once preparation is complete.

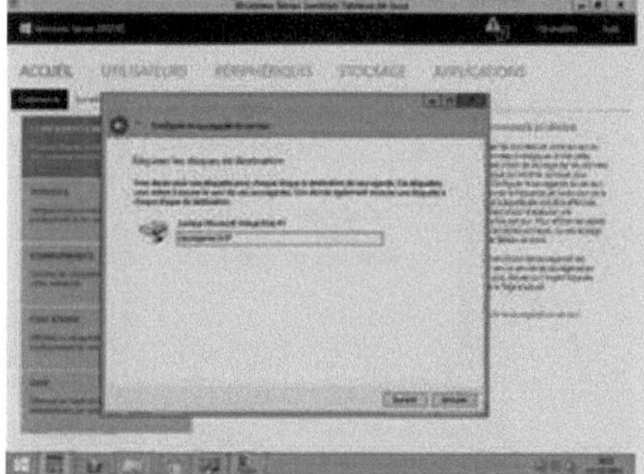

Definition of backup planning.

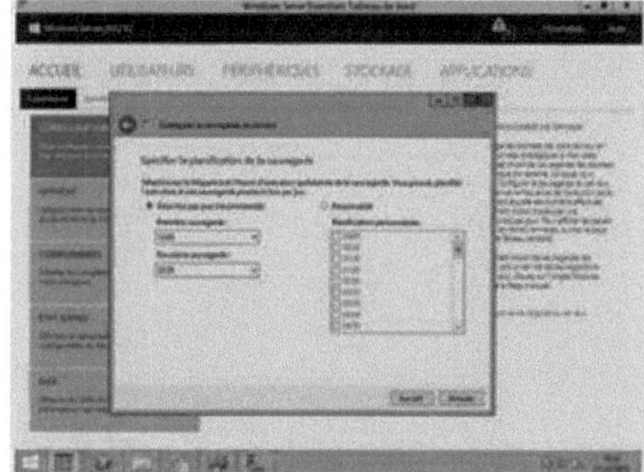

Select the items to be saved.

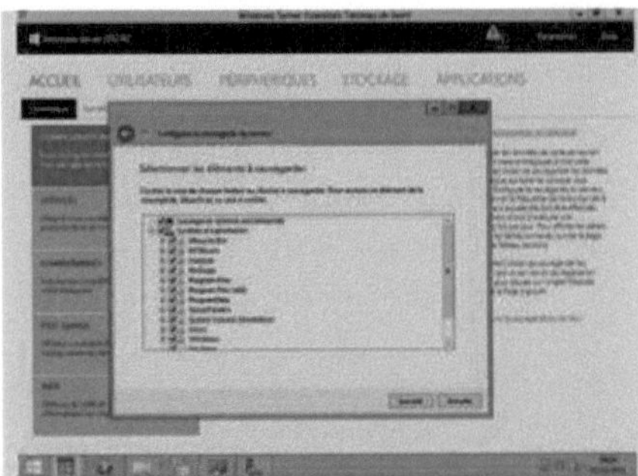

Apply the settings and launch the configuration.

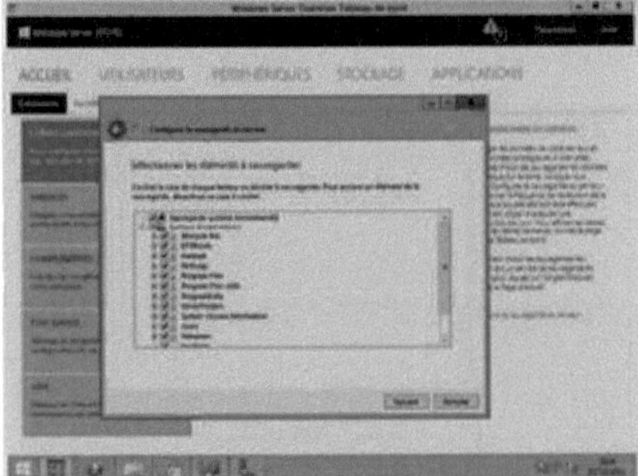

The backup configuration is complete.

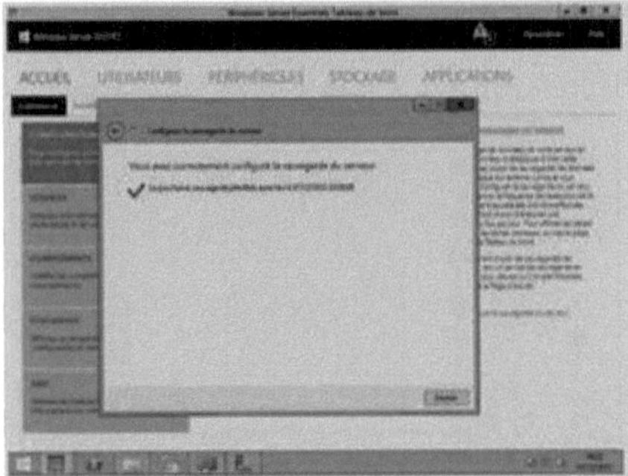

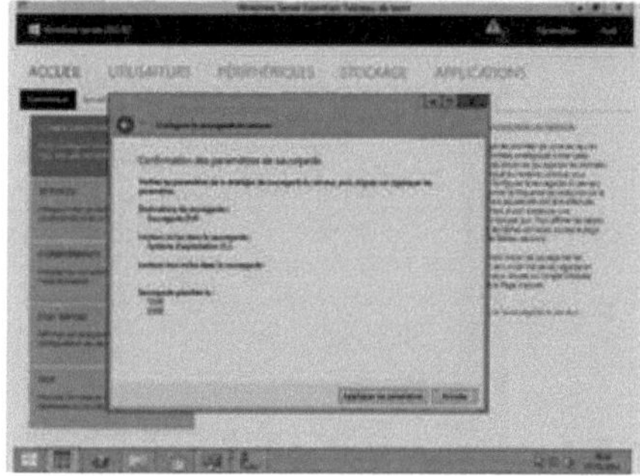

CREATING A NETWORK SHARE

Once on the server dashboard :

Load the wizard by clicking on "configure access anywhere".

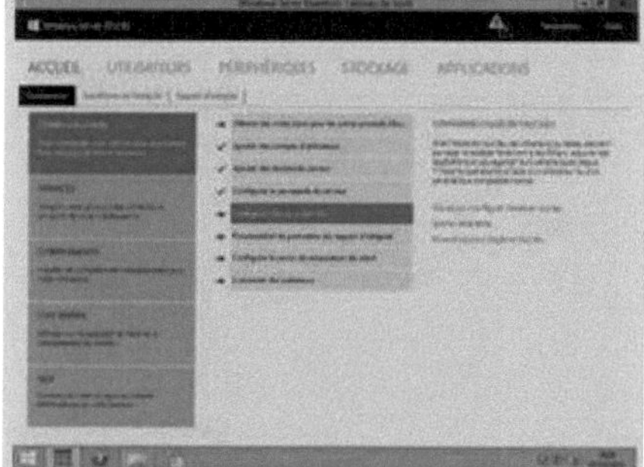

Open the wizard.

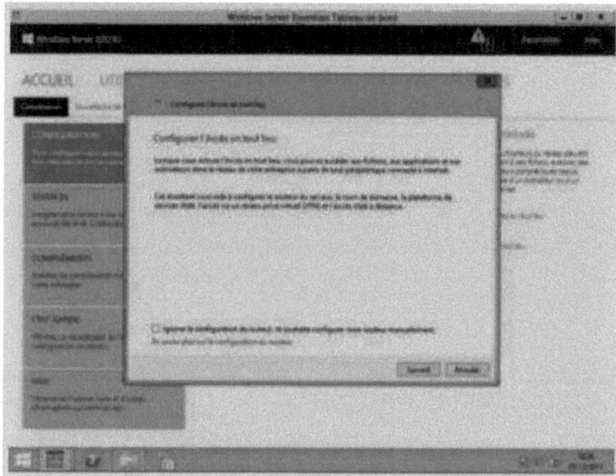

Choose an option for configuring the domain: There are two possible choices, and we recommend that you choose option 2^{e} as it is free and does not require you to purchase a certificate.

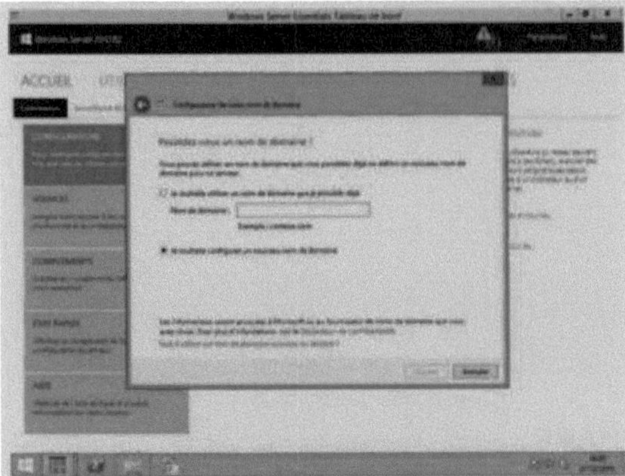

Log in with your Microsoft account.

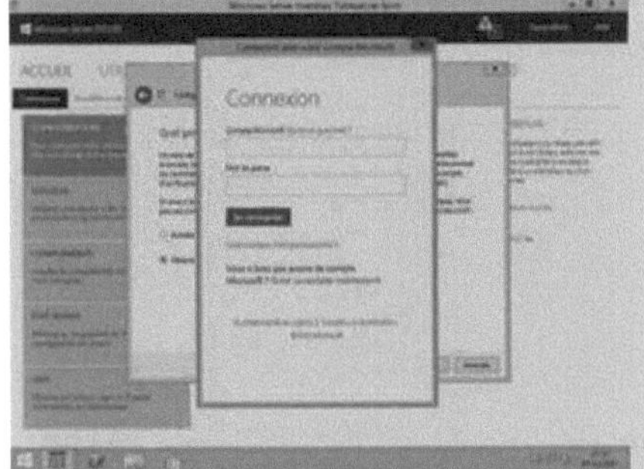

Creating your domain name.

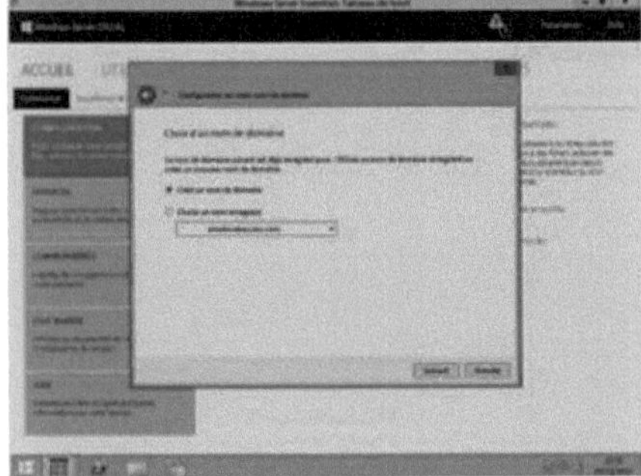

Wait until the domain name registration is complete.

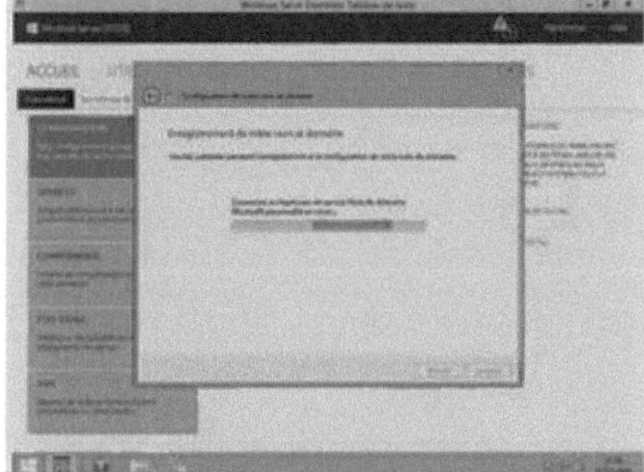

The domain is configured.

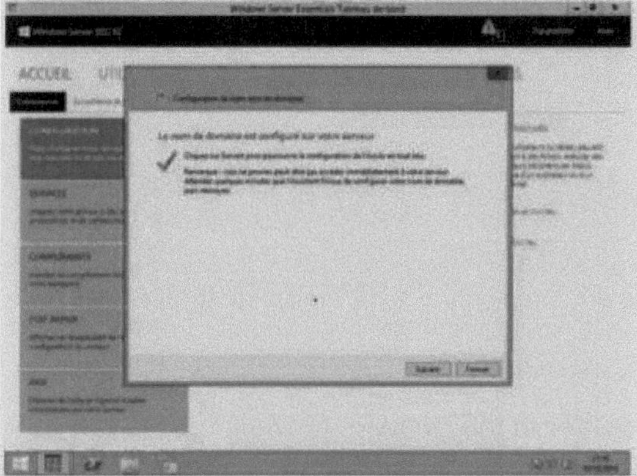

Activate access functions anywhere.

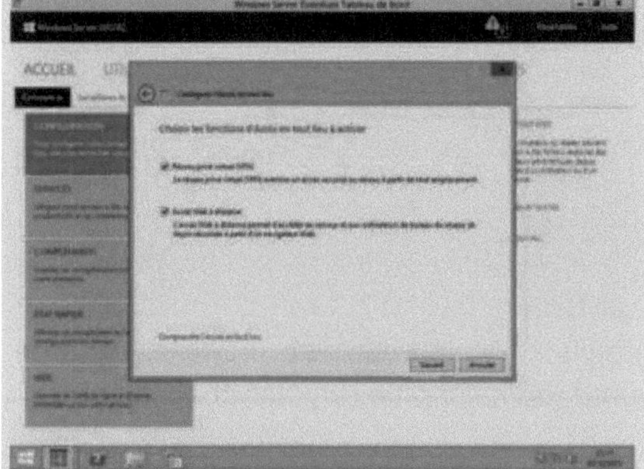

Authorise this access.

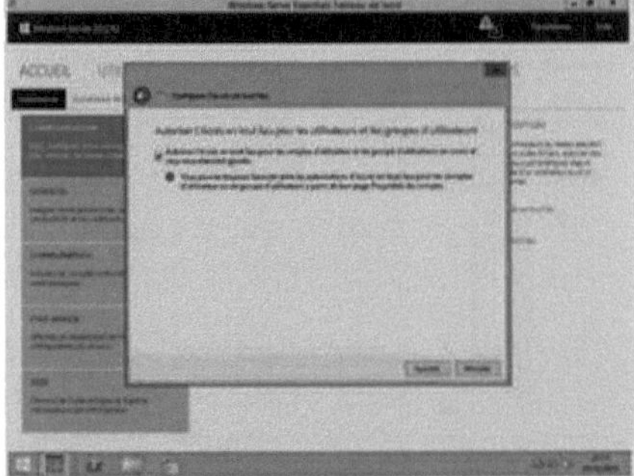

Continue configuring the new parameters.

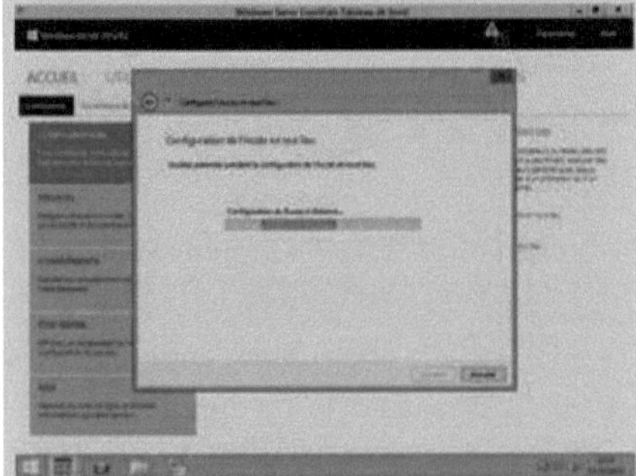

Authorise publication of the server in the network firewall.

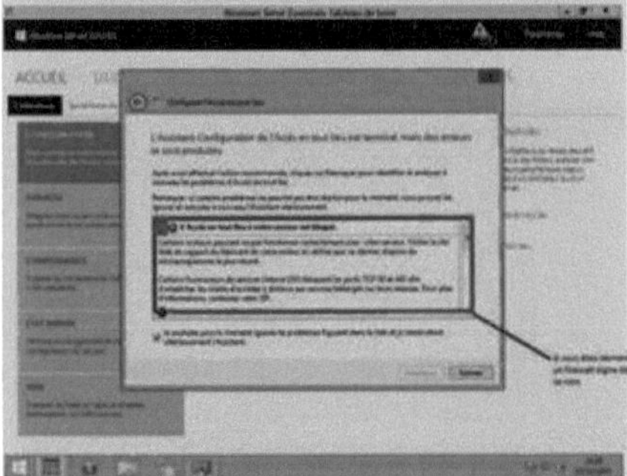

Once the configuration is complete, go to your web browser and enter the address you have configured (domainname.remotewebacess.com).

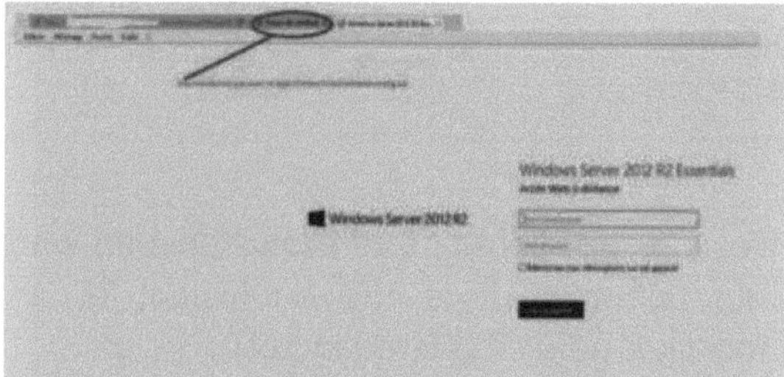

Once you have logged in, you will be taken to your interface.

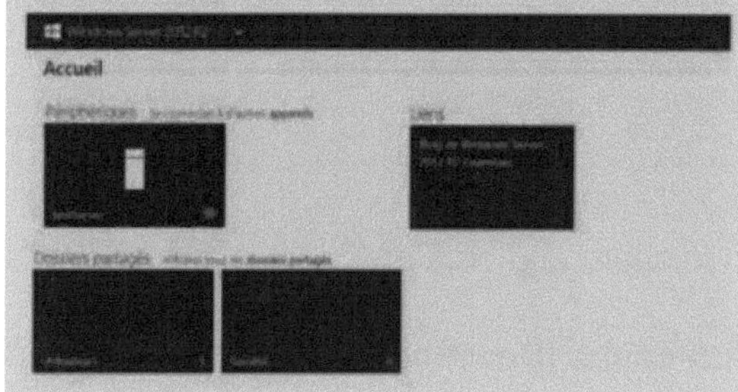

IV.12.SHARING DIGITAL LIBRARY DATA

The 'Drive' storage space makes it easy to share resources with one or more users, inside or outside the school. 4 types of sharing are available:

. **Download link**: an alternative to cumbersome 'attachments' or the 'filex' service

. **Send link**: a way for your correspondents to upload files to one of your folders.

- **Sharing with a user**: a shared space with a user.

An equivalent to "shared directories".

- **Sharing with a group**: a shared space with a group of users, created in your 'Drive' storage space.

You can view, modify or delete all your shares and links on the page.

on the home page of your Drive space, from the [My shares] section (located in the banner on the left of your space).

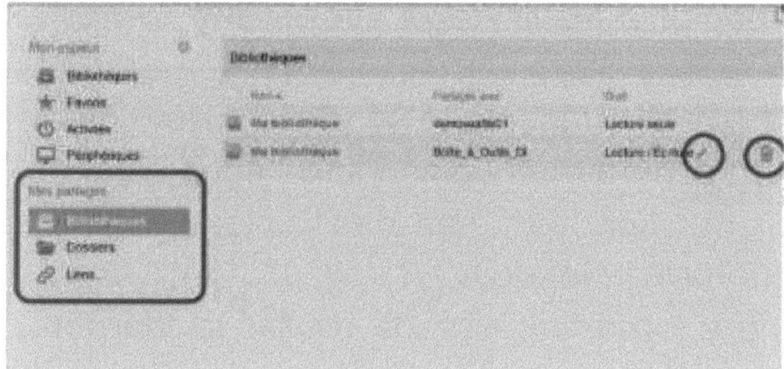

By hovering over a share, you can :
. modify associated rights (pen icon)
• delete this share (bin icon).

DOWNLOAD LINK

A download link points to a file, folder or library, and allows anyone who has the link to download its contents. It is the equivalent of an 'attachment' in an email, like the 'filex' service offered in ENT.

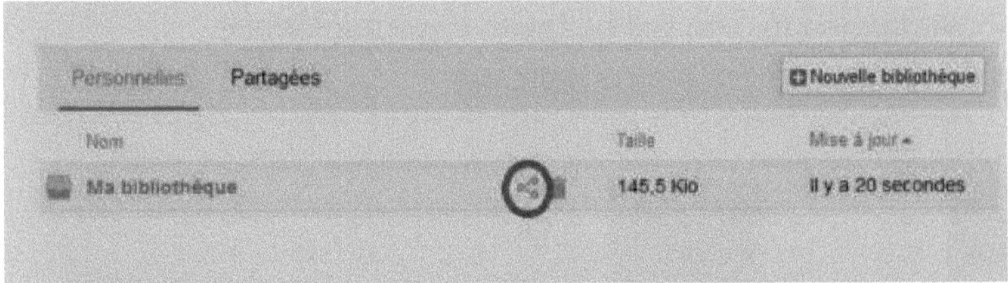

1. Choose the item you wish to share and click on the share icon.
2. A new window opens. Click on the [**Download link**] button. You can then choose to add a password and/or an "expiry" date to the share. Click on the the button [**Generate**] button.

You can then send the share link to the users concerned using the [**Send**] button or your email software (by copying the link displayed on the interface).

Please note: You can [**Delete**] the generated link at any time. The share will then become inactive and no-one will be able to access its content. If you wish, you can generate a new share link at a later date.

3. (Optional) If you set a password, clicking on the [**Magic Wand**] icon will automatically generate a password.
4. (Optional) We recommend that you specify the number of days during which the link will remain active. Once this period has elapsed, the link will be automatically deactivated and no-one will be able to download the attached resource.

SENDING LINK

A send link points to a folder or a library and allows any owner of this link to send files to it.

Example: I'm a teacher and I ask my students to send me a file. I create a folder in my Drive space and generate an upload link. I send them this link by email. By clicking on this link, they can each upload their file, without seeing what the others have uploaded.

The procedure for generating a send link is quite similar to that for a download link:

Select the folder or library => Icon [**Share**] ==> Button [**Send link**] ==> Add a password if required ==> Button [**Generate**] => Button [**Send**] (or send the link address using your own email software).

SHARE WITH A USER

Sharing with a user allows you to share one or more libraries or folders with a user **who has already connected** to their Drive storage space. This is the equivalent of a "shared directory".

This user will then have access to the content of the share and will be able to upload files and modify them if you give them "**Read/Write**" rights.

To share a library or folder with a user, simply follow the steps below:

Selecting the folder or library ==> [**Sharing**] icon ==> [**Share with user**] button ==> Searching for the user (using all or part of their name or e-mail address) ==> Choosing the rights allocated to the share ==> [**Submit**] button.

SHARING WITH A GROUP

Sharing with a group allows you to share one or more libraries or folders with members of a group that has been created beforehand in your Drive space. The procedure is very similar to that described in the section on sharing with a user:

Selecting the folder or library ==> [**Sharing**] icon ==> [**Share with a group**] button ==> Searching for the group (using all or part of its name) ==> Selecting the rights allocated to the share ==> [**Submit**] button.

CHAPTER V

SOCIAL NETWORKS

V .1. DEFINITIONS OF CONCEPTS

V .1.1.SOCIAL NETWORK

A social network is a website that allows Internet users to create a personal page to share and exchange information, photos or videos with their community of friends and acquaintances.

V .1.2.DIGITAL IDENTITY

Digital ID is a key technology that simplifies and secures access to various online services. It allows users to connect to multiple sites without having to create multiple accounts and passwords.

V .1.3.SAFETY

Social media security involves **a set of policies and procedures used to protect users' information, privacy and accounts on various social networking sites**. It provides security against online harassment, unauthorised access, phishing attacks, malware, data breaches and identity theft.

V .1.4. CONFIDENTIALITY

Confidentiality on a social network means that **the perpetrators of violence will not have access to your profiles**. This won't stop them from publishing information about you on their own pages or those of others.

V .2. TYPES OF SOCIAL NETWORKS

Its a safe bet that when you hear the term 'social networks', you think directly of Facebook, Instagram, LinkedIn or Twitter. However, social networks bring together a variety of different social platforms that meet a wide range of needs. Each offers opportunities for content publishers and businesses to increase their visibility and achieve their objectives. Understanding the diversity and plurality of social media helps to put in place the best communication and acquisition strategy.

V .2.1. SOCIAL NETWORKS (FACEBOOK, LINKEDIN AND TWITTER _)

The best-known social networks are Facebook, Linkedin and Twitter.

Social networks are clearly the most popular social media with the general public, or are the first to be mentioned when we list the main types of social media. Social networks connect individuals, businesses and other entities to each other. They encourage the sharing of knowledge and are all about personal interaction between individuals or with brands, for example.

Users can share ideas, organise content, upload photos and videos, form groups based on their interests and take part in discussions. They are built around the user and everything that is important to them and their 'social circles'.

Social networks enable companies to achieve a variety of objectives:

- ❖ Strengthen their brand image
- ❖ Gaining visibility
- ❖ Connecting with their target
- ❖ Optimising customer relations and conversion
- ❖ Create links with individuals or companies

V.2.2.CONTENT SHARING PLATFORMS (INSTAGRAM, YOUTUBE...)

The best-known content-sharing platforms are Instagram, Youtube and Snapchat.

Content sharing networks are used to find and share photos, live videos and other types of media on the web. Visual content such as images, infographics and illustrations more easily capture the attention, imagination and emotion than other social media. Social media platforms such as Instagram, Imgur and Snapchat are designed to amplify the power of image sharing. Users create, organise and share unique images that spark conversation. An image is worth a thousand words for your business. They offer individuals and brands a place to discover and share media so that target audiences can be engaged and converted in a compelling, results-driven way. These days, social networks also offer these features.

Content sharing platforms enable companies to achieve a variety of objectives:

- Gain visibility
- Creating emotion and commitment
- Enhancing brand content
- Generate leads
- Strengthen your brand image

SOCIAL BOOKMAKING AND CURATION NETWORKS

The social bookmaking and curation networks are Pinterest and Flipboard.

Bookmarking and curation networks help people to discover, save and share quality content. They are the preferred channels for ideas, news, topical issues and current trends. They are very useful for finding out about brand awareness for your company and the content it produces. What's more, choosing them to run different types of social media marketing campaigns will help you generate website traffic and customer engagement. If you want to launch creative campaigns that can not only inform your audience but also attract them, this is the best solution.

To launch a social networking campaign on Pinterest, you need to have a site that is compatible with bookmarking. You need to optimise the titles and images of the feeds that bookmarking and content curation networks use to access and share your content. Flipboard allows you to create your own Flipboard magazine using the most engaging content, then you can present it to your audience.

Bookmarking and curation networks enable companies to achieve a variety of objectives:

. Distributing quality content

. Enhancing visual brand content

- Generate traffic
- Creating engagement with your brand
- Active monitoring

V.3.ROLES

Social networks came into being well after the advent of websites and e-mail, to enable users to share photos/videos, memories, and even more stories and opinions with everyone they know simultaneously (group message) over unmeasurable distances (across borders). They therefore form communities that communicate and exchange written and audiovisual information.

All it will take is a penny to get a data connection and be able to communicate with a long-lost friend or family member, or close a business deal .

Further afield, social networks are not just about sustainable communication (communicating constantly with someone thousands of miles away), they are also about marketing and sales. We'll be talking about sales groups and business pages for companies.

V.4.BENEFITS

The reason why social networks are attracting so much attention is that they are the key to communication in our society, whatever your age. It's a virtual revolution that we've been watching grow for over twenty years. Here are the main **advantages of social networks**:

- **Solidarity**

First and by no means least, social networks are a great way of **developing solidarity**, whether it's posting a recommendation, looking for people, humanitarian causes or finding good deals.

- **Combating isolation**

More and more people are feeling lonely in an individualistic society. These social exchange platforms enable lonely people to reconnect with family and friends, or to **create virtual friendships** that can lead to real encounters.

For business

The development of this network is a godsend for getting the word out about your small business. You can advertise your business for free or at low cost. You can **boost your publications** by targeting your audience for just a few euros a day. Which is no mean feat when you consider how difficult it is to find customers.

- **Professional exchange**

We have seen that LinkedIn is the most suitable **social media** for jobseekers. With the ability to create your CV online and distribute it to potential employers, LinkedIn is considered to be the most professional network. As well as being registered with Pole emploi and various other platforms, the LinkedIn social network will be very useful for engaging in an exchange with an employer.

You can also send messages directly (called inmail) with a LinkedIn Premium subscription. The first month is free for new users. So you can try it out! Discover our online training courses. L'Ecole Franqaise **is a certified training organisation** that offers online training courses. They can be financed by mutualised vocational training funds.

- **Networking**

Whether you're an author, artist, craftsman, salesperson or jobseeker, there's no need to go door-to-door to make yourself known. Networking is all about expanding your virtual network through publications that are shared by your contacts. Expanding your network adds value to your business.

❖ **Creating a community**

Do you have a talent that you want to share with targeted people? Thanks to social networks, you can surround yourself with people who are just like you. Share, create, broadcast, collaborate and communicate around a theme in a Facebook group. For Twitter, it's the short text or image that is highlighted in the group, like, for example, sharing a link or a news item.

❖ **Generate traffic to your site or blog**

A tip for **increasing the visibility of your site** or blog: simply create an eye-catching publication inviting your contacts to click on the link and sign up for the newsletter. You can also publish one of your blog posts on the social networks and add a link to it. Always be active, offer games for example, the key is to bring your contacts to your site or blog. In conclusion, social networks are a major asset to our social lives. They have become everyone's favourite **means of communication**. By staying at home, you can catch up with old friends, reconnect with family and make new friends. The use of social media is also common in the professional world, because it develops networking. What's more, it opens the door to market research.

V.5.DISADVANTAGES

Before embarking on the social media arena, bear in mind that its advantages can also be accompanied by disadvantages. Here are just a few of them.

❖ **A waste of time**

Have you ever logged on to a company's Facebook profile and found that it had not been updated for three years? Doesn't that make you feel abandoned? Don't let your sites look like tumbleweed in a Western film.

Maintaining a social network - and even more so if it's not just one, but several - requires dedication. If you want your company's profile to be alive, to y have user participation and to give the impression of not being abandoned, you'll need to update it frequently, feed it with content, respond to messages from your users... All this takes time and effort, so you'll need to assess whether it's worth it, bearing in mind that having a profile and not looking after it can be counter-productive.

❖ **They may require a financial investment**

As well as taking time and effort, the person in charge of managing your social networks needs to be qualified to do so (your cousin Paco who has just finished a macrame course may not be the right person). The need for competence in this area is so great that, in recent years, a new

profession (community manager) has emerged, devoted mainly to it.
Bear in mind that if you want your social media profiles to look like they're not run by amateurs, you may have to put your hand in your pocket.

❖ **Creating boring content that only talks about your company's good points**

Would you often visit a company's profile if all they did was tell you over and over again that they were the most beautiful, the most intelligent and that their products were the best? Nobody likes a narcissist (except themselves). **Make sure you bring value to your customers;** launch offers, publish interesting content (articles, for example), answer questions, etc.

❖ **Negative advertising**

Just as social networks can provide you with great doses of good publicity for your business, be aware that they can also expose your company's sins. To avoid this, you can do two things: 1) Always give the best possible service (which will ensure that your customers have no reason to speak ill of your company) and 2) Handle your customers' complaints well, giving a satisfactory resolution or response that turns them into praise.

❖ **Your problems will be more visible**

If you accept all kinds of comments on your social media profiles, or even use them to respond to queries and complaints, they will be much more exposed to the world. Keep in mind, and if you decide to do it, give it your best shot so that your users and potential customers can see that you know how to solve problems.

❖ **Exposing yourself to trolls**

Even if you give your users the best possible response, you will sometimes come across people who are not your customers, but who simply want to have fun at your expense. These are the famous "trolls" of the Internet. In some circles, it's said that "if you have a troll, you have a treasure", but this is much more unlikely in the business world, so you'll have to learn to deal with them.

❖ **♦♦ You could get in trouble for extortion**

As annoying as they can be, trolls aren't the worst thing that can happen to you on social media. Although it's not very common these days, it has happened in the past and continues to happen today; some companies have been victims of extortion from customers - and even non-customers - asking for all sorts of benefits (discounts, gifts and even some money) in exchange for not posting negative comments on social media. I hope you never have to go through that!

- **You may experience confidentiality or security problems**

In some cases, social media can be an open door to information about your company or your customers that you should keep well hidden. Be careful, it can get you into serious trouble.

- **Competitors can study you**

Just as in our article on the advantages of social networks for businesses we told you that they were a good way of finding out about the competition, you have to imagine that the competition also has eyes and could use them for the same purpose. To do better than them...

Here are just some of the disadvantages that social networking can present for businesses. Some of them can be avoided, but bear in mind that you can't control everything that happens on the internet, so others will be inevitable, and you may even have to deal with them if you don't have a social media profile or site. Anyway, good luck!

V.6. NETWORK SAFETY ISSUES

Attackers often use social network accounts during the reconnaissance phase of a social engineering or phishing attack. Social networks can provide attackers with a platform to impersonate trusted individuals and brands and obtain the information they need to carry out other attacks, including social engineering and phishing.

V.6.1.DOU RISKS ON SOCIAL NETWORKS?

The methods used by an attacker depend on the social networking platform targeted.

Facebook allows users to keep their images and comments private, so an attacker will often friend a target user's friends or send a friend request directly to a target user to access their posts.

If an attacker can connect to several friends of the target user, the latter is more likely to accept the friend request depending on the number of friends connected.

LinkedIn is another common social networking target. LinkedIn is known for its business networks, and users' networks are usually filled with colleagues and other employees from the same organisation.

If an attacker is targeting a company, LinkedIn is an excellent social networking site for collecting professional emails for a phishing attack. A large company may have several networked employees who list their employer and title.

An attacker can use this public information to find several employees who have access to financial information, private customer data or high-privilege network access.

Collecting information to steal data is not the only reason to use social networks for reconnaissance. Information published on social networks can be used to obtain passwords or impersonate professional users.

Many online accounts allow users to reset their password if they enter a security question. With enough information from social network posts, an attacker could guess the answer to these security questions based on the private information posted by a target user.

Brand spoofing is another threat posed by social networks.

With enough information gathered, an attacker can impersonate a commercial brand to trick users into sending money, divulging private information or providing account credentials.

Attackers also use this threat to carry out cross-site scripting (XSS) or cross-site request forgery (CSRF) attacks. These attacks can lead to more massive data breaches and the compromise of commercial infrastructures.

WHAT DOES A THREAT ON SOCIAL NETWORKS LOOK LIKE?

Since many social networking platforms display users' messages publicly, attackers can silently collect data without users' knowledge. Some attackers go further to gain access to user information by contacting target users or their friends.

The way in which an attacker implements a threat on social networks depends on his objectives.

If an attacker is looking for a high-stakes reward, the best way to quickly obtain a monetary reward for their efforts is to target companies. An attacker might first consult LinkedIn for a list of possible targets. Targets can be a mix of high-level corporate employees and low-privilege users who might be tricked into sending additional corporate data or falling for a phishing attack that gives the attacker access to account credentials.

Armed with a list of targets, an attacker can then examine social network accounts in search of personal information. Personal information can help the attacker gain the target's trust in a social engineering attack. It can also be used to guess the answers to security questions in order to take control of the account or to get closer to a user with greater privileges. Pet names, favourite sports teams and study history are all potential clues to passwords or answers to questions used to verify the user's identity in order to reset a password.

Once the attacker has gathered all the necessary data, the next step is to launch the attack. An attacker can use one of the following methods:

. **Social engineering.** An attacker can call employees to entice them to send private data, prove their identity or pay him money. In the case of a complex attack, the attacker can impersonate a high-level executive to trick the target user into transferring money to the attacker's account.

. **Phishing.** An attacker can use information gathered on social networks to impersonate the sender of an email message and trick users into clicking on links or sending private data to the attacker. The email address of a high-level employee can be spoofed by a message asking the recipient to send money, click on a malicious link or reply with sensitive data.

- **Brand identity theft.** By using the names of a brand's employees, the attacker can trick customers into believing that requests come from the legitimate brand. This can be used to trick users into disclosing personal information or account credentials.
- **Site compromise and data theft.** With enough information from social networks, an attacker can write malware explicitly targeting the company or carry out an attack to gain access to the internal network where the attacker can then exfiltrate data.
- **Malware propagation.** As with identity theft, a hacker can create domains and websites that pretend to be the legitimate company and trick users into downloading malware or providing credentials.
- **Data leakage.** If a hacker gains access to an account's credentials, this could lead to a major breach of corporate data.

Given that there are several social networking platforms on the Internet, a hacker can practice social engineering and phishing using a variety of threat methods. There is no single threat to an attacker on social networks.

But recognition and basic research using social networks are the same. Any public information on private or professional social network accounts can be used for other attacks.

PROTECTING YOURSELF AGAINST RISKS ON SOCIAL NETWORKS

Most threats on social networks come from employees who publicly disclose too much private and professional information. As these accounts are personal, companies cannot prevent users from being present on social networks. But they can educate users on the best ways to protect their data and their identifiers.

Education is essential to put an end to the risks on social networks. Individuals can educate themselves, but companies need to set up training programmes for every employee so that they can detect and prevent social engineering and phishing.

The first step is to make users aware of the dangers of disclosing too much information online to the public. Even social network accounts defined as private can be used as part of an attack if the attacker gains access to private feeds.

Users should never post private company information on their social network accounts or information that could be used as part of a takeover of the account.

Some organisations distribute mobile devices and allow users to install social networking applications. These companies must provide an acceptable use policy that determines what users can post using the company's devices.

It is also essential to protect these devices from malware to prevent the company's social networking accounts from being hacked.

Remote wiping software must be installed if an employee physically loses their device or if it is stolen.

V .7. CREATION OF A PLATFORM(GROUP)

We will refer to this as the Whatsupps platform or Whatsupps group.

V .7.1.STARTING A WHATSAPP GROUP: FIRST STEPS

Our increasingly digital age is fostering new ways of connecting through instant messaging applications, and WhatsApp is no exception.

Thanks to its extremely popular groups, sharing ideas and communicating have never been easier.

V .7.2.GROWING POPULARITY OF WHATSAPP GROUPS

WhatsApp has a unique charm in the modern world, combining the advantages of a messaging application with the organisational flair of groups.

V .7.3.ADVANTAGES OF WHATSAPP GROUPS

- WhatsApp groups are much more than just chat rooms. With member restrictions, extended capabilities, photo sharing and messaging, they offer powerful and practical communication.

V.7.4.THE IMPORTANCE OF EFFECTIVE GROUP MANAGEMENT

- New groups thrive on appropriate guidance, order and user etiquette. Learning how to create and manage WhatsApp groups helps strengthen social ties and encourages the emergence of an online community.

V.7.5.WHATSAPP GROUP CREATION PROCESS

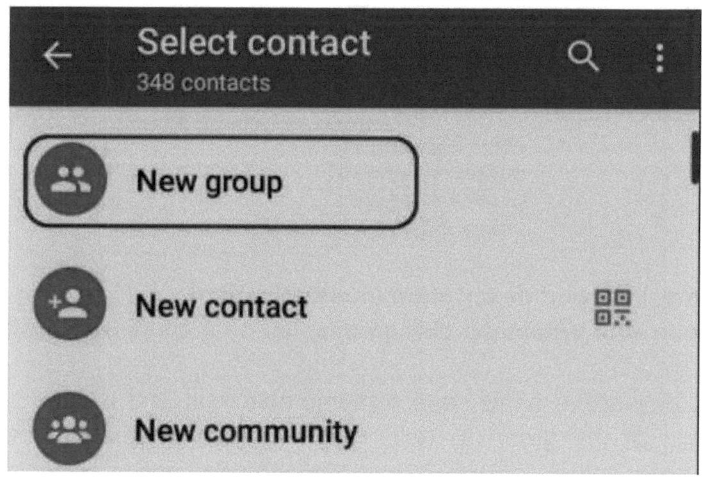

- Step 1: Open WhatsApp.
- Step 2: Go to the Cats menu.
- Step 3: Create a new group.
- Step 4: Select the contacts.
- Step 5: Add details and create the group.

V.7.6.STEPS TO FOLLOW BEFORE CREATING YOUR WHATSAPP GROUP

Before you set about creating your WhatsApp community, make sure you follow these essential steps to ensure the success of your group:

1. Check compatibility: Check your device settings and confirm that your WhatsApp version is up to date.
2. Backup of contacts and chat history: Secure your data by continuously backing up your contacts and chats in the cloud or on a local storage platform.
3. Gather the data needed to create the group: Determine the group's objective and the types of interaction desired, as well as the choice of participants.
4. Set membership criteria: Create a criteria for admitting members that helps maintain the group dynamic in a spirit of collaboration and efficiency.

V.7.7.MANAGING YOUR WHATSAPP GROUP: 3 ESSENTIAL STEPS

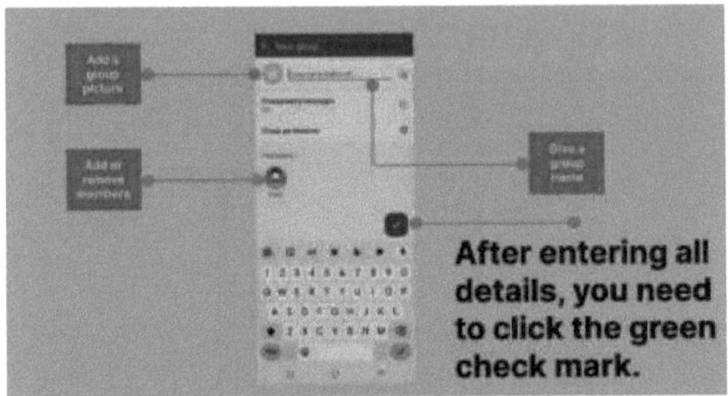

1. **Group name, icon and description (customisation)**

Find the group in your WhatsApp discussions, tap on it and select "Edit group details".

Enter a clear, descriptive name, add a memorable icon and include a brief description of the group to help new members understand its purpose.

2. **Definition of member authorisations**

Once you have personalised the group identity, access the "Group settings" and change the permissions if necessary. These may include

. Restrict the ability to send messages to group administrators only, or allow all members to contribute.

- Grant or revoke the right to modify group information.

3. **Welcome and introduction**

V .7.8.MAKING YOUR WHATSAPP GROUP UNIQUE

FIND OUT ABOUT MEMBERS' PRIVILEGES

Once you've created your group, it's essential to understand how members engage with it.

WhatsApp grants administrators and members different levels of privileges. Administrators have full control, while other members have more limited capabilities.

V .7.9. CONFIGURING GROUP DETAILS

Access the group settings to change names, add photos or update descriptions. By making the subject of your group attractive, members are more likely to stay engaged.

V .7.10.CHOOSING BETWEEN SILENT AND NOISY NOTIFICATION PARAMETERS

Customise notifications to adjust alert behaviour, allowing both quieter conversations and louder exchanges, depending on the preferences of group members.

V .7.11.TIPS FOR MANAGING CAT PARAMETERS

Unclutter your group chat by hiding untidy conversations or pinning important discussions to the top of the screen. These options can improve the functionality and engagement of the group.

V .7.12.MEMBERSHIP MANAGEMENT AND COMMUNICATION

V .7.12.1.HOW TO INVITE YOUR CONTACTS TO THE GROUP

1. Create a new group on WhatsApp with up to 1024 participants.
2. Press "New group" on the "Chats" screen.
3. Select the contacts you want or search for new ones.

V.7.12.2.GUIDE TO ADDING AND DELETING GROUP MEMBERS

1. Go to the group information page and press "Add a participant".
2. You can also share the group invitation link with other people.
3. Delete participants by selecting "Delete a participant".

V.7.12.3.HANDLE MEMBERS' REQUESTS CORRECTLY

1. For Android: Tap on the name of the group, choose "Group info", then "Add participants".
2. For iPhone: Swipe left on the group discussion, select "More" and tap "Add participants".

V.7.12.4.HOW TO START A GROUP CONVERSATION

1. Create a group subject and enter the key information.
2. Share photos, videos and documents to keep everyone interested.
3. Use polls, reader card responses and the "Reply" function to manage discussions.

CONCLUSION

The rapid growth and popularity of WhatsApp provides a golden opportunity to form micro-communities and foster a connected environment, which is why it's so important to learn how to create WhatsApp groups.

Identifying WhatsApp's powerful attributes, such as broad usability, robust sharing features and ease of management, ensures that the digital age of communication is constantly evolving and user-centric.

TimelinesAI, a business-focused WhatsApp management solution, aligns seamlessly with the growing demand for organised and effective communication methods such as WhatsApp group chats. If you're interested in the idea of creating WhatsApp groups and managing them effectively, especially from a business perspective that aims to promote collaboration between teams and improve communication with customers on WhatsApp, TimelinesAI is a service worth considering.

By providing comprehensive and efficient features such as a shared inbox for multiple numbers and seamless CRM integrations, it cultivates an advanced communication paradigm, unlocking a whole new level of business performance on WhatsApp.

V.8. ETHICS AND MORALITY TO BE OBSERVED ON SOCIAL MEDIA

Social networks have transformed the way we communicate, work and play. They have made it possible to forge links between people around the world, but they have also raised complex ethical issues. This section examines the main ethical issues associated with social networks, including privacy, freedom of expression, misinformation, cyberbullying and the impact on mental health. We will also analyse the responsibilities of companies and users in the face of these challenges and the prospects for a more ethical use of social networks.

1. PRIVACY AND DATA PROTECTION

Protecting privacy is a major issue on social networks. Users often share personal information, such as their location, job, interests and relationships, without always understanding the privacy implications. Social network companies collect and use this data to personalise advertising and improve the user experience. However, this practice raises ethical questions about consent, transparency and the misuse of data.

Data protection is also a major ethical issue. Data breaches, such as those affecting Facebook and LinkedIn, have exposed the personal information of millions of users. Companies must therefore put in place robust security mechanisms to protect their users' data and be transparent about their data collection and use practices.

2. FREEDOM OF EXPRESSION AND CONTENT MODERATION

Freedom of expression is a fundamental right, but it can come into conflict with other values, such as respect for human dignity and the fight against discrimination. Social networks are often criticised for their handling of hateful, discriminatory or violent content. Companies need to strike a balance between protecting freedom of expression and preventing abuse.

Content moderation is a complex ethical issue. Automated moderation algorithms can be biased or make mistakes, while human moderation can be costly and stressful for moderators. Companies need to invest in more effective and ethical moderation solutions, and involve users in defining moderation rules.

3. DISINFORMATION AND FAKE NEWS

Disinformation and fake news spread rapidly on social networks, undermining trust in institutions and the media. Companies need to take steps to combat misinformation, for example by checking facts, reporting misleading content and reducing its visibility. Users also have a role to play by checking sources and sharing reliable information.

4. CYBERBULLYING AND ONLINE HARASSMENT

Cyberbullying and online harassment are major ethical problems on social networks. It can have devastating consequences for the mental health of victims and lead to tragic situations. Companies have a responsibility to combat this behaviour by putting in place reporting and moderation mechanisms, and by punishing the perpetrators of harassment.

Users must also be aware of the impact of their actions online and behave respectfully towards others. Awareness campaigns and educational programmes can help to promote a culture of respect and empathy on social networks.

5. THE IMPACT ON MENTAL HEALTH AND WELL-BEING

Excessive use of social networks can have a negative impact on people's mental health and well-being. Social networking can lead to social comparison, addiction, reduced self-esteem and a waste of valuable time. Companies have a responsibility to encourage healthy use of their platforms, for example by limiting notifications and promoting time management tools.

Users also need to be aware of their use of social networks and put in place strategies to preserve their well-being, such as setting time limits, disconnecting regularly and focusing on offline activities.

6. THE RESPONSIBILITIES OF COMPANIES AND USERS

Social network companies have a responsibility to put in place policies and mechanisms to manage the ethical issues described above. They must be transparent about their practices, comply with current regulations and work with governments, civil society organisations and users to improve the ethics of their platforms.

Users also have a role to play in behaving ethically and responsibly on social networks. They must respect the rules of the platforms, be aware of the impact of their online actions and contribute to creating a safe and respectful online environment.

7. PROSPECTS FOR A MORE ETHICAL USE OF SOCIAL NETWORKS

To promote more ethical use of social networks, there are several possible avenues of development:

1. Strengthening the regulation of social networks, particularly in terms of data protection, content moderation and the fight against disinformation.

2. Promoting media and information literacy to develop users' critical thinking and sense of responsibility.

3. Encourage companies to adopt business models that are less based on the collection and use of personal data.

4. Encourage cooperation between companies, governments, civil society organisations and users to develop common ethical standards and share best practice.

5. Raising users' awareness of the ethical issues involved in social networking and encouraging them to adopt responsible and respectful behaviour.

The ethical issues surrounding social networks are complex and interdependent, involving both companies and users. Protection of privacy, freedom of expression, disinformation, cyberbullying and the impact on mental health are all challenges that need to be met to ensure responsible and ethical use of social networks.

To achieve this, it is essential to strengthen regulation, educate users, encourage companies to adopt more ethical business models and promote cooperation between the various players involved. By working together, we can help to create a safer, more respectful and ethical online environment, where social networks can be used in a positive and beneficial way for all.

CHAPTER VI

IT SECURITY

V I.1.DEFINITIONS OF CONCEPTS

V I.1.1.VIRUSES

A virus is a malicious computer program designed to disrupt the normal operation of a computer system without the owner's knowledge.

V I.1.2.ANTIVIRUS

An antivirus is a security program designed to prevent, detect, scan for and remove viruses and other types of malicious software from computers, networks and other devices.

V I.1.4.CUSTOMER

A computer client is a computer or application that sends requests to a server.

V I.1.5.BLANKET

A firewall is a computer network security system that limits Internet traffic entering, leaving or within a private network.

This software or dedicated hardware-software unit works by selectively blocking or allowing packets of data. It is generally intended to help prevent malicious activity and to prevent anyone, inside or outside a private network, from engaging in unauthorised web activity.

Firewalls can be thought of as boundaries or gateways that manage the movement of authorised and prohibited web activities within a private network. The term comes from the concept of physical walls that act as barriers to slow the spread of fire until the emergency services can extinguish it. In comparison, network security firewalls are designed to manage web traffic: generally to slow the spread of web threats.

Firewalls create 'bottlenecks' to channel web traffic, which are then examined against a set of programmed parameters and acted upon accordingly. Some firewalls also track traffic and connections in audit logs to reference what has been authorised or blocked.

Firewalls are generally used to block the boundaries of a private network or its host devices. As such, firewalls are a security tool within the broader category of user access control. These barriers are generally set up in two places: on the network's dedicated computers or on the computers of the users and other terminals themselves (hosts).

VI.1.5.1.OPERATION OF FIREWALLS

A firewall decides what network traffic is allowed through and what traffic is deemed dangerous. Essentially, it works by filtering the good from the bad, or the reliable from the unreliable. However, before going into detail, it is useful to understand the structure of networks on the Internet.

Firewalls are designed to secure private networks and the terminal devices they contain, known as network hosts. Network hosts are devices that "communicate" with other hosts on the network. They send and receive data between internal networks, as well as outgoing and incoming data between external networks.

Computers and other terminal devices use networks to access the Internet and other equipment. However, the Internet is segmented into sub-networks for reasons of security and confidentiality. The basic sub-network segments are as follows:

1. **External public networks** generally refer to the public/global Internet or various extranets.
2. **The internal private network** defines a home network, company intranets and other "closed" networks.
3. **Peripheral networks** are border networks made up of *bastion hosts*: computer hosts dedicated to enhanced security capable of withstanding an external attack. As a secure buffer between the internal and external networks, they can also be used to host all the outward-facing services provided by the internal network (i.e. servers for the Web, mail, FTP, VoIP, etc.). They are more secure than external networks but less secure than internal networks. *They are not always present in simpler networks such as home networks, but can often be used in company or national Intranets.*

Filtering routers are specialised gateway computers placed on a network to segment it. They are known as home firewalls at network level. The two most common segmentation models are the host filter firewall and the subnet filter firewall:

- **Filter host firewalls** use a single filter router between the external and internal networks. These networks form the two sub-networks of this model.
- **Filtering subnet firewalls** use two filtering routers: one known as the *access router* between the external network and the edge network, and another known as the *retention (or "choke") router* between the edge network and the internal network. This creates three sub-networks, respectively.

Both the network perimeter and the host machines themselves can house a firewall. To do this, the firewall is placed between a single computer and its connection to a private network.

- **Network firewalls** involve the application of one or more firewalls between external networks and internal private networks. They regulate incoming and outgoing network traffic, separating external public networks, such as the global Internet, from internal networks such as home Wi-Fi networks, corporate Intranets or national Intranets. Network firewalls can take the form of one of the following types of device: dedicated hardware, software and virtual.

- **Host-based firewalls** or "software firewalls" involve the use of firewalls on individual user devices and other private network terminals as a barrier between network devices. These devices, or hosts, provide customised regulation of traffic to and from specific computer applications. Host-based firewalls can run on local devices as an operating system service or as a terminal security application. Host-based firewalls can also take a closer look at web traffic, filtering based on HTTP and other network protocols, allowing you to manage the content that arrives on your machine, rather than where it comes from.

A network firewall needs to be configured to accommodate a wide range of connections, whereas a host-based firewall can be tailored to the needs of individual machines. However, host-based firewalls require more customisation effort, which means that network firewalls are ideal for a complete control solution. But using both types of firewall at both sites simultaneously is ideal for a multi-layered security system.

Filtering traffic through a firewall uses pre-established or dynamically learned rules to allow and deny connection attempts. These rules control how a firewall regulates the flow of web traffic through your private network and private computing devices. All firewalls, regardless of type, can filter through a combination of the following elements:

- **The source:** where an attempted connection comes from.
- **The destination:** where a connection attempt is supposed to go.
- **Content:** what a connection attempt is trying to send.
- **Packet protocols :** The "language" used by a connection attempt to transmit its message. Among the network protocols that hosts use to "talk" to each other, TCP/IP protocols are mainly used to communicate on the Internet and within Intranets/subnetworks.
- **Application protocols:** common protocols include HTTP, Telnet, FTP, DNS and SSH.

The source and destination are communicated by Internet Protocol (IP) addresses and ports. IP addresses are unique device names for each host. *Ports* are a sub-level of any given source and destination host device; they are similar to the different rooms in a large building, for example. Ports are generally assigned for specific purposes, so certain protocols and IP addresses using uncommon ports or inactive ports may prove problematic.

Using these identifiers, a firewall can decide whether a data packet attempting to connect should be rejected, silently or with an error response to the sender, or forwarded.

VI.1.5.2.TYPES OF FIREWALL

Different types of firewall incorporate different filtering methods. Although each type has been developed to outperform previous generations of firewalls, much of the core technology has been passed down from generation to generation.

Firewall types differ in their approach to the following elements:

1. Connection tracking
2. Filtering rules
3. Audit logs.

Each type operates at a different level of the standard communications model, the Open Systems Interconnection (OSI) model. This model gives a clearer picture of how each firewall interacts with the connections.

V I.1.5.2.1.STATIC PACKET FILTERING FIREWALL

Static packet filtering firewalls, also known as stateless inspection firewalls, operate at the OSI network layer (Layer 3). They provide basic filtering by checking all individual data packets sent over a network, according to their origin and destination. In particular, previously accepted connections are not tracked. This means that every connection must be re-approved with every data packet sent.

Filtering is based on IP addresses, ports and packet protocols. These firewalls, at the very least, prevent two networks from connecting directly to each other without authorisation.

Filtering rules are defined on the basis of a manually created access control list. They are very rigid and it is difficult to cover undesirable traffic appropriately without compromising network usability. Static filtering requires constant manual revision to be effective. This may be feasible on small networks but can quickly become difficult on larger ones.

The inability to read application protocols means that the content of a message delivered in a packet cannot be read. Without reading the content, packet filtering firewalls offer limited protection.

V I.1.5.2.2.GATEWAY FIREWALL AT CIRCUIT LEVEL

Circuit-level gateways operate at session level (layer 5). These firewalls check whether the packets are working when a connection is attempted and, if they are working properly, they allow a permanent open connection between the two networks. The firewall then stops supervising the connection.

Apart from its approach to connections, the circuit-level gateway can be similar to proxy firewalls.

The permanent unmonitored connection is dangerous, because legitimate means could open the connection and then allow a malicious actor to enter unhindered.

V I.1.5.2.3.FIREWALL WITH DYNAMIC INSPECTION

Stateful inspection firewalls, also known as stateful packet filtering firewalls, differ from static filtering in their ability to monitor connections in progress and remember connections that have been made. They started out operating at the transport layer (layer 4), but today these firewalls can monitor many layers, including the application layer (layer 7).

Like static filtering firewalls, stateful inspection firewalls allow or block traffic based on technical properties, such as specific packet protocols, IP addresses or ports. However, these firewalls also uniquely track and filter based on the state of connections using a state table .

This firewall updates the filtering rules according to the connection events recorded in the status table by the filtering router.

In general, filtering decisions are often based on the administrator's rules when configuring the computer and the firewall. However, the state table allows these dynamic firewalls to make their own decisions based on previous interactions that they have 'learned' from. For example, traffic types that have caused disruption in the past will be filtered out in the future. The flexibility of stateful inspection has made it one of the most widely used types of protection.

V I.1.5.2.4.PROXY FIREWALL

Proxy firewalls, also known as application-level firewalls (Layer 7), have the unique ability to read and filter application protocols. They combine application-level inspection, or "deep packet inspection (DPI)", with dynamic inspection.

A proxy firewall is as close to a real physical barrier as it's possible to get. Unlike other types of firewall, it acts as two additional hosts between the external networks and the internal host computers, with one of them acting as a representative (or 'proxy') for each network.

Filtering is based on application-level data rather than IP addresses, ports and basic packet protocols (UDP, ICMP) as in packet-based firewalls. Reading and understanding the FTP, HTTP, DNS and other protocols enables deeper investigation and cross-filtering for many different data characteristics.

Like a security guard at the entrance to a building, it essentially examines and evaluates incoming data. If no problems are detected, the data is authorised to be transmitted to the user.

The disadvantage of this type of enhanced security is that it sometimes interferes with incoming data that does not pose a threat, resulting in operational delays.

VI.1.5.2.5.NEW GENERATION FIREWALL (NGFW)

The evolution of threats continues to demand more intense solutions, and new-generation firewalls remain at the forefront of this problem by combining the functionality of a traditional firewall with network intrusion prevention systems.

Next-generation threat-specific firewalls are designed to examine and identify specific threats, such as advanced malware, at a more granular level. More frequently used by enterprises and sophisticated networks, they offer a complete solution for filtering threats.

VI.1.5.2.6.HYBRID FIREWALL

As its name suggests, the hybrid firewall uses two or more types of firewall in a single private network.

VI.1.7.NETWORK SECURITY

Network security encompasses all activities aimed at protecting the functionality and integrity of your network and your data.

. It includes hardware and software technologies

. It targets a large number of threats

- It prevents them from penetrating the network or spreading.

V I.1.7.1.NETWORK SECURITY OPERATIONS

Network security combines many layers of defences at the edge and within the network. Each layer of network security implements policies and controls. Authorised users gain access to network resources, while malicious actors are blocked from carrying out their exploits and threats.

V I.1.7.2.HOW TO MAKE THE MOST OF NETWORK SECURITY

Digitalisation has transformed our world. Our way of living, playing and learning. Everything has changed. Every company that wants to offer the services its customers and employees demand needs to protect its network. Network security also helps you protect your proprietary information from attack. Basically, it protects your reputation.

V I.1.8.CYBERCRIME

Cybercrime is a general term describing the myriad of criminal activities carried out using a computer, network or other set of digital devices.

Cybercrime covers a wide range of illegal activities committed by cyber criminals. These include hacking, phishing, identity theft, ransomware and malware attacks, among many others.

The scope of cybercrime knows no physical borders. Criminals, victims and technical infrastructures can be found all over the world. With the use of technology to exploit security vulnerabilities, both by individuals and businesses, cybercrime takes many forms and is constantly evolving.

The ability to effectively investigate, prosecute and prevent cybercrime is an ongoing battle with many dynamic challenges.

Cybercrime poses a serious threat to individuals, businesses and government entities, and can result in significant financial loss, damage to reputation and compromise of records.

As technology advances and more and more people use digital devices and networks for their day-to-day activities, the threat of cybercrime continues to grow, making it more important than ever to take steps to protect against it.

VI.1.8.1.TYPES OF CYBERCRIME AND EXAMPLES

Cybercrime covers a wide range of criminal activities involving various digital platforms and technologies.

There are many types of cybercrime worth tackling, from email scams and social networking activity to phishing scams and ransomware attacks.

Although some of these offences overlap, the most common are as follows:

1. Email scams

These are deceptive manoeuvres that take many forms. Fake emails mislead recipients, while social engineering techniques trick people into divulging information, such as credit card numbers, or transferring money to the attacker.

Phishing schemes, in which fraudsters imitate legitimate brands, are a common form of email scam.

2. Fraud on social networks

Scams that use social networking platforms such as Facebook, Twitter, Instagram and TikTok to deceive and defraud victims. Examples include bogus online shops, catfishing, social engineering attacks and identity theft scams.

Social network fraud often exploits users' trust, naivety and tendency to share too much personal information online.

3. Bank fraud

Fraudulent activities targeting financial institutions or their customers and stakeholders. Banking fraud most often results in significant financial loss or identity theft, and attackers' strategies often involve sophisticated hacking and social engineering tactics.

Examples include credit card fraud, ATM rip-offs and online banking scams.

4. E-commerce fraud

An elaborate scam that exploits the weaknesses and pitfalls of online shopping technologies, such as fabricated online shops, fake seller accounts or the theft of credit card information.

Cases of e-commerce fraud generally result in financial losses for both consumers and online retailers.

5. Malware

A widespread software attack designed to damage and manipulate computer systems by introducing viruses, Trojan horses or spyware.

Malware is a widespread problem, targeting both individual PCs and corporate computer networks. They are most often used to disrupt networks and steal user data.

6. Ransomware

A type of malware attack that encrypts victims' critical data and demands payment of a ransom in exchange for a decryption key to regain access.

Financially crippling for individuals and organisations alike, ransomware attacks often result in the loss of data and assets, tax devastation and disruption to productivity.

One of the most high-profile cases of ransomware involved the Costa Rican government, leading to a national emergency.

7. Cyber espionage

The use of hacking, malware attacks or other cybernetic activities in which an unauthorised user attempts to gain access to sensitive data or intellectual property in order to gain a competitive advantage over a company or government entity.

Cyber espionage cases often involve state-sponsored groups or individual hackers and can have major political or economic implications.

One of the most significant cases of cyber espionage is that of the five Chinese military hackers charged with hacking, economic espionage and other offences targeting US entities.

8. Data breaches

Unauthorised access or leakage of sensitive data, such as confidential information, critical records or financial access.

Data breaches can be attributed to a wide range of risk factors, such as weak passwords and cyber security protocols, software system vulnerabilities or internal threats.

The consequences can be compromised data, financial damage or a tarnished reputation. Verizon's data breach investigation report found that 82% of breaches involved a human element.

9. Computer viruses

This is perhaps the most common type of malware, capable of replicating itself and spreading to other systems, often causing damage to files or computer programs. The Melissa, ILOVEYOU and Nimda viruses are examples of computer viruses that spread rapidly to infect files and damage computer systems.

10. DDoS attacks

Distributed Denial of Service attacks, or DDoS attacks, are designed to overwhelm a network or website with traffic, causing it to slow down or fail completely.

DDoS attacks are one of Russia's many destructive cyber activities against Ukraine, along with other attacks aimed at deleting computer data belonging to government and private entities.

11. Software piracy

Digital form of intellectual property theft involving the unauthorised use or distribution of copyrighted material, such as software, music or films. Examples of software piracy include the use of key generators or crack software to activate paid-for software without a licence.

12. Phishing

Email fraud using techniques such as deceptive emails, fraudulent websites or misleading communications to trick victims into sharing their personal information and sensitive data or clicking on links to malicious downloads and websites.

Examples of phishing scams include emails that appear to come from well-known brands, financial institutions, government agencies or social networking sites.

13. Identity theft

In a digital context, identity theft refers to the acquisition of a person's private data for fraudulent or malicious purposes.

Assets targeted by identity theft include social security numbers, date of birth, credit card details or online accounts.

Types of identity theft include financial, medical and tax identity theft, identity theft on social networks and identity cloning, where someone uses another person's identity to conceal their own.

14. Online harassment

Cyberbullying, cyberharassment and repeated acts designed to frighten, hurt, anger or shame a particular person.

Today, online harassment is most prevalent on social networking sites, dating applications and forums/messages. Examples of online harassment include the sending of inappropriate and unsolicited messages, clear and intentional threats, or the dissemination of sensitive photos or videos of a victim.

15. Cyberterrorism

These are generally larger acts of online destruction, using the internet or computer technology to commit acts of terror, for example by causing infrastructure damage and catastrophic disruption, stealing confidential information or disseminating propaganda with political or cultural implications.

Cases of cyberterrorism are becoming more and more sophisticated, which increases the demands made on cyber security and protection.

V I.1.8.2.THE IMPACT OF CYBERCRIME

The growing sophistication of cybercrime is accompanied by an increase in the volume of threats and associated financial losses. According to FBI reports, Secretary Mayorkas of the Department of Homeland Security said that losses from cybercrime would exceed $4.1 billion by 2020.

More recent reports from the FBI's Internet Crime Complaint Center (IC3) division indicate that losses will exceed $6.9 billion in 2021. According to the IC3 report, the FBI attributes this sharp rise in cybercrime-related losses to an increase in ransomware attacks, corporate email compromise scams and cryptocurrency-related crimes.

The report also highlights the changing landscape of cyber attacks, which are increasingly linked to international relations and threats from foreign intelligence services.

At a more granular level, cybercrime pervades the homes and personal computers of many people. According to statistics from the Cyber & Infrastructure Security Agency (CISA), 47% of Americans have exposed their personal information to online criminals, and malware has infected a

third of personal computers.
The future impact of cybercrime appears to be a key economic driver and a massive call to action for cyber security companies and the countries that host them.
Cybersecurity Ventures predicts that the global cost of cybercrime will continue to rise by 15% per year over the next five years, reaching $10.5 trillion in annual damages by 2025.

V I.1.8.3.PREVENTING CYBERCRIME

As the overall costs and risks associated with cybercrime continue to rise, so too does the need to implement, monitor and constantly improve prevention systems and technologies. Between foreign adversaries, terrorists and everyday crooks, cyber attacks are becoming increasingly intelligent and sophisticated.
Individuals, businesses and government entities must take proactive measures to prevent cybercriminals from penetrating security systems and infiltrating sensitive data .
While certain cybercrime prevention strategies remain unstoppable in repelling attackers, a new wave of modern technologies has come to support these initiatives.

V I.1.8.4.ADVANCED CYBER SECURITY SYSTEMS

One of the main strategies for preventing cybercrime is to use advanced cyber security protection.
These include fundamental technologies such as firewalls, anti-virus software and intrusion detection systems, but also more advanced cyber security systems that are evolving thanks to artificial intelligence (AI) and machine learning (ML).
Implementing the right cyber security tools should be an absolute priority for any organisation or individual wishing to protect themselves against cyber attacks and digital threats.

1. Multifactor authentication

Multi-factor authentication (MFA), commonly known as two-factor authentication, is a common security protocol that prevents data breaches, hacking and other direct cyber attacks.
In simple terms, this process requires users to provide at least two forms of identification to authenticate access to their accounts, for example a password and an access code sent to a device.
Now a best practice protocol for organisations, MFA adds extra layers of cyber security to online accounts, making it much harder for hackers to access your data.

2. Virtual private networks

A virtual private network (VPN) is a service that allows users to surf the Internet with greater security and anonymity.

VPNs are designed to encrypt online activity, making it much more difficult for cyber-attackers to intercept and steal your data. VPNs act as intermediaries between your device and the target server, adding their own layer of encryption and routing communications through their own servers.

VPNs are particularly effective in helping to protect against email fraud such as phishing by masking your IP address and location.

V I.1.8.5. EMAIL SECURITY SOLUTIONS

Email accounts are one of the channels most frequently exploited by cyber-attackers to gain access to sensitive data and private information.

Specialised email security technologies can be used to prevent this activity, including solutions such as email encryption, spam filters and anti-virus software.

Encryption is a powerful technology that protects the content of emails from interception.

Spam filters detect and prevent unwarranted and malicious emails from reaching your inbox, while anti-virus software detects and removes malicious email attachments.

V I.1.8.6.PASSWORD MANAGERS

Cybercriminals frequently attack passwords. As well as creating secure passwords that are difficult to crack, password managers are software applications that securely store multiple login credentials in an encrypted database, all locked behind a master password.

Password managers are commonly used by organisations, remote teams and individuals to provide extra protection when browsing the web, while keeping passwords in a secure space.

The most common password managers are 1Password, KeePass, LastPass and Apple's iCloud Keychain. However, some password managers present risks.

V I.1.8.7.SAFETY AWARENESS TRAINING

Many cyber attacks are the result of human error, such as clicking on malicious links or downloading files containing viruses.

Security awareness training aims to teach users how to better identify, avoid and mitigate the threat of cyber attacks. The most common forms of training are computer-based awareness training and phishing simulation exercises, where employees receive fake phishing emails to test their reaction.

Security awareness training helps organisations instil a culture of security, creating a more resilient network to protect against cyber-attackers.

V I.1.8.8.DATA BACKUP AND RECOVERY

Many forms of cyber attack can result in the loss of critical data, which can have serious financial and operational repercussions for both individuals and organisations.

Data backup and recovery solutions can help mitigate the damage caused by data loss by creating backup copies of data and ensuring faster recovery in the event of a ransomware attack, data breach or other form of cyber attack.

Regular archiving of data is an essential security protocol to guarantee the recovery of your data in the event of an attack.

V I.1.8.9. PROTECTION AGAINST CYBERCRIME BY IA AND ML

The most advanced cybercrime prevention technologies now use machine learning and artificial intelligence to collect and analyse data, track and trace threats, identify vulnerabilities and respond to breaches.

For example, machine learning algorithms can detect and prevent fraud in financial transactions by identifying patterns that indicate fraudulent activity and flagging them for review.

Similarly, IA technologies can detect and prevent cyber attacks on networks and systems by analysing network traffic, identifying anomalous patterns and responding to threats in real time.

V I.1.9.CYBER ATTACK

Cyber attacks are aimed at damaging, taking control of or gaining access to important documents and systems within a corporate or personal network.

Cyber attacks are carried out by individuals or organisations for political, criminal or personal gain, with the aim of destroying or gaining access to sensitive information.

Here are a few examples of cyber attacks:

. Malicious programs
- Distributed denial of service (DDoS) attack

. Hameponnage
- SQL code injection attack
- Cross-site scripting (XSS)
- Botnet

. Ranpongiciels

Using reliable software and a solid cyber strategy can reduce the chances of a corporate or personal database being affected by a cyber attack.

VI.1.9.1.DIFFERENT TYPES OF CYBER ATTACKS AND THREATS

Cyber attacks target computer networks and systems, and take a variety of forms. Malware and phishing are two examples of cyber attacks used to take control of sensitive corporate data and personal electronic devices. Find out more about the types of cyber attacks and their effect on recent technologies.

VI.1.10.CYBER SECURITY

Cyber security involves protecting computers, servers, mobile devices, electronic systems, networks and data from malicious attacks. It is also known as computer security or information systems security. You can find it in many contexts, from corporate computing to mobile terminals. It can be divided into several categories.

- **Network security** involves protecting the computer network against intruders, whether targeted attacks or opportunistic malware.
- **Application security** aims to protect software and devices from threats. A corrupt application could open up access to the data it is supposed to protect. A reliable security system can be identified at the design stage, well before a programme or device is deployed.
- **Information security** ensures the integrity and confidentiality of data, whether stored or in transit.
- **Operational security** includes the processes and decisions involved in processing and protecting data. User authorisations for access to the network and the procedures that define the storage and location of data come under this type of security.
- **Disaster recovery and business continuity** specify how a business responds to a cyber security incident or other event causing a loss of business or data. Disaster recovery policies govern the way in which a business recovers its operations and information to the same operating capacity as before the event. Business continuity refers to the plan on which a company relies while trying to operate without certain resources.

. **End-user training** focuses on the most unpredictable factor: people. Anyone can accidentally introduce a virus into a normally secure system by not following good security practices. Teaching users to delete suspicious attachments and not to plug in unidentified USB sticks is essential for a company's security.

VI.1.11.HACKING

Hacking is the process of modifying a system or device so that it runs a different operating system to the one originally intended. Hackers use their knowledge and skills to exploit vulnerabilities in software, hardware and networks to gain access to resources or information that would not otherwise be available.

Hackers also often use hacking tools such as viruses, **spyware** or Trojan horses, as well as **social engineering** techniques such as **phishing** emails, which try to persuade users to provide them with information that they should not have access to.

VI.1.11.1.THE DIFFERENT TYPES OF HACKING

There are several types of hacker: white hat, black hat and grey hat.

White hat hackers are people who use their computer skills to good effect, for example to find security holes in software or websites and fix them before someone else exploits them maliciously.

Black hat hackers use their knowledge for criminal activities such as identity theft or stealing confidential credit card information from unsuspecting online users.

Grey hats are somewhere in between: they can sell their services to both parties depending on which one offers them the most money or fame at any given time! They can use 'black hat' techniques for laudable purposes, and conversely, 'white hat' techniques for malicious purposes.

Ethical hacking is another term used to describe someone who uses their technical skills to test an organisation's IT security systems without being paid by the organisation (which is basically another way of saying 'white hat').

Corporate Hacking refers specifically to employees of a company attempting to gain unauthorised access to company networks or computers without the permission of members of management in order to test security protocols.

Is hacking illegal?

Piracy is not illegal, only the purpose is. Hacking itself is not a crime, but using it to steal information or cause damage can be. For example:

- If you hack into someone's email account and read their private messages without their permission, that's illegal, because it's an invasion of privacy.
- If you use your skills as a hacker to break into someone else's computer system so that they can no longer access (or even delete) their own files, this is a computer crime and is illegal in most cases. The same

goes for any other type of hacking that deprives someone else of access to their property or causes damage by attacking their network infrastructure (such as wifi routers).

VI.1.12.CRACKING

Cracking, or hacking, goes further. **Cracking refers to any hacking of a security system for malicious or criminal purposes.** The person who commits it is therefore a cracker, or pirate. Just as a thief opens a bank safe by manipulating the combination, a hacker uses his technical skills to break into a computer, a programme or an account.

Most of the media, and consequently most people, use the terms 'hacking' and 'hacker' to describe this kind of activity. But in the world of hacking, we prefer to use the term 'cracking' for this kind of malicious hacking, which we'll simply call 'piratage' here.

Cracking refers to the hacking of a security system for malicious or criminal purposes.

The methods used are often less sophisticated than hacking techniques, which is another reason why people who define themselves as "hackers" distance themselves from this more prosaic and egotistical type of activity. Hackers who rely exclusively on tools developed by others are known as "script kiddies", or "teenage hackers".

VI.1.12.1.THE MOST COMMON TYPES OF PIRACY

It is often said that hackers create and pirates destroy. The aim of hacking is to gain access to places or systems to which the hacker does not normally have access, for malicious purposes such as **data theft, identity theft or the free use of paid software**. Let's take a look at some common types of hacking.

Password hacking

Password hacking consists of obtaining a password from data stored somewhere. Any website or service with a modicum of security will encode the passwords it has by **hashing**. This is a one-way process that takes the password, transforms it using a given hashing algorithm and then saves the encrypted password. The fact that this is a one-way process is an important point: as a result, **the hash is not reversible.** When a user tries to log in, the password they enter is also transformed by hashing, and if the two hashed passwords are identical, the user is authorised to access their account.

To guess the password, the hacker must first recover the hashed data from the website. This happens much more often than you might think, as websites are very often hacked. Next, the hacker needs to know the exact combination of hashing algorithms, as well as all the other techniques the website uses to hash passwords.

Once armed with these two pieces of information, he can get to work. But as the hash is not reversible, the hacker has no choice but to try and reproduce this hash. They generate a password, hash it, then check whether it matches an existing hash. This operation is time-consuming if carried out manually, so the hacker uses specialised programmes and powerful computers capable of producing a very large number of results per second. Brute force and dictionary attacks, as well as rainbow table attacks, are the most common methods of password hacking.

- **Brute force:** the algorithm produces random strings of characters until it finds the right one.
- **Dictionary:** similar to the brute force method, but instead of using random characters, the dictionary method is limited to existing words.
- **Rainbow table:** the rainbow table uses pre-calculated hash values to try to determine the encryption used to hash the password.

VI.2. SOME VIRUSES AND ANTIVIRUSES

VI.2.1.SOME EXAMPLES OF THE BEST-KNOWN COMPUTER VIRUSES

1. ILOVEYOU: the fatal attachment

We're starting with a great classic that dates back to the early 2000s and has already claimed millions of victims around the world. Although the practice is well known, some naive Internet users don't hesitate to **open the attachment to an email** sent by a friend, entitled Love-Letter-for-you.txt.vbs. But they've got it all wrong! As soon as it was opened, the worm hidden in the attachment **modified the computer's files and accessed the address book** to send itself to contacts. As a result, the user's computer slows down considerably!

2. CryptoLocker: the "ranqongware that's going to fleece you

Just as you turn on your computer to check your emails, a message appears on your screen with a **countdown timer**. You still have a few hours to **pay a ransom to regain access** to your data or it will be **destroyed**! The most famous of these, CryptoLocker, has been around since 2013.

3. JIGSAW: you have one hour to pay

The JIGSAW virus is particularly dangerous in that it gives its victim just one hour to **pay the required ransom** before starting to delete files. The rate of destruction then increases little by little with each passing hour, **until all the disks have been emptied** in just 72 hours.

4. **PETYA: the virus that encrypts your data**

This ransomware **targets businesses in particular**, and completely paralyses the operation of its victims' computers or computer networks by encrypting their data and system files. **PETYA** is aware that this virus can prevent companies from continuing their business activities, and the **ransoms demanded** to restore the situation are often very high.

5. **LOCKY: the most widespread ransomware**

The LOCKY virus directly targets files with certain **extensions on the hard disk**, and French and German Internet users are highly exposed. Like the 2 previous viruses, this type of *ransomware* **encrypts the** targeted files to prevent access, while deleting internal backups to block any attempt at recovery. The data is then immobilised until a ransom of several thousand euros is paid to obtain the access keys.

6. **Heartbleed: your passwords are no longer confidential**

You had finally decided to **swap your password for a code** that you yourself had trouble remembering, but that wasn't enough in the face of Heartbleed. This virus allows hackers to recover small pieces of code from secure servers, and even **reconstitute complete passwords**. If your twittosphere is informed overnight of all your latest drinking sprees, then Heartbleed is the culprit.

7. **Freak: watch out for your bank account**

FREAK uses a **security flaw in the TLS protocol**, the main mechanism for securing communications on the Internet. Once the encryption has been 'broken', hackers can spy on the infected PC's communications and **install malicious software**. In the wrong hands, it can, for example, connect to your online bank account and empty it in the blink of an eye!

8. **Stuxnet: the anti-nuclear worm**

Stuxnet is one of the **most dangerous computer worms** ever discovered. Conceived by the NSA in collaboration with Unit 8200 (an intelligence unit of the Israeli Defence Force) to attack **Iranian** uranium enrichment **centrifuges**. Capable of altering the speed at which the machines rotate, until they are destroyed, in 2010 it was used to cause the simultaneous failure of all the **uranium enrichment centrifuges** that were to be used to create a nuclear bomb in Iran. Scary!

9. **Regin: the cyber-spy virus**

Regin is a veritable **cyber espionage platform**, allegedly created by the National Security Agency and its British counterpart, the Government Communications Headquarters (GCHQ). Its main role is to collect data and it can **take total control of target computers**. It can spy on telephone conversations, retrieve emails, see live what is being written on a computer, take screenshots, steal passwords, etc. Active since 2008, it is believed to have been used to **spy on European institutions** and the telecommunications company Belgacom. Private companies, government entities or research institutes: it's all for Regin!

10. Waledac: the leading spam botnet

The **massive spam mailings for viagra** that we've all experienced are the cause of *botnets.* These computer programmes perform the same task repeatedly. With almost 1.5 million messages sent every day, Waledac is without doubt **one of the most painful botnets** ever conceived. After months of tracking it down, Microsoft eradicated it in 2010, but since then new, far more sophisticated botnets have emerged and are still emerging. Now, instead of relying on a central server, hackers use a **mesh of networks**, with virtual machines in charge of sending spam.

Only an up-to-date **antivirus** can protect your computer against all these attacks. We can only advise you to get a good antivirus, whether it's for your **computer, your smartphone or even your tablet**!

VI.3. CAUSES AND EFFECTS OF COMPUTER VIRUSES ON DATA, FILES, SOFTWARE AND COMPUTER NETWORKS

Detecting a computer virus can be tricky, as viruses often try to remain hidden. However, certain signs can indicate that your computer is infected and reveal what viruses can do to your computer:

SIGNS OF POTENTIAL INFECTION BY A COMPUTER VIRUS :

. **Slower performance:** If your once-responsive computer suddenly runs slowly and tasks take longer than usual, this could be a sign that a hidden virus is exploiting your system's resources, reducing its speed and responsiveness.

- **Pop-up windows or unwanted messages:** An influx of pop-up windows or persistent error messages that disrupt your digital experience may indicate the infiltration of malware.

. **Frequent crashes or lock-ups :** If your computer is prone to frequent crashes or unexplained freezes, the presence of a virus could be the cause, orchestrating disruptions that interrupt your workflow and undermine your productivity.

. **Browser changes:** Unauthorised changes to your web browser settings or unexpected changes to your home page indicate potential viral interference. A virus or other malware can manipulate your online activity and affect your digital autonomy.

• **Missing or corrupted files:** The sudden disappearance of files or the discovery of corrupted data can reveal the destructive capabilities of a virus. Viruses can delete or manipulate files, resulting in loss of data or software malfunctions that impair the operation of your system.

. **Strange network activity:** An unexpected increase in your Internet usage may be a worrying sign that a virus is using your network to connect to its command server. The activity of this clandestine network highlights the need for a rapid and thorough investigation.

• **Disabled security software:** Some clever viruses disable your antivirus software, rendering it powerless against their onslaught. If you find that your security software is mysteriously deactivated, exercise caution as your system could be at serious risk.

• **High CPU usage:** If you check your computer's Task Manager (or Activity Monitor on macOS) and see abnormally high CPU usage, it could mean that a virus is operating surreptitiously in the background. High CPU usage can indicate that a virus is running malicious processes out of your sight.

If you notice any of these warning signs, it is essential that you act quickly to identify and remove the virus. Use Norton AntiVirus Plus to run a full system scan to identify and remove any viruses or other malicious code.

VI.7.DOWNLOADING FREE ANTIVIRUS SOFTWARE FROM THE NET

A. androT de

How do I download and install a free antivirus application for Android? It's very simple: here's how to download a free antivirus application, like Avast Mobile Security: **Access the Google Play Store here. Download the security application to your device by clicking Install**.

B. PC

To use a free antivirus, **you need to visit the website of the antivirus and antimalware tool of your choice, click on the download link and follow the installation instructions.**

VI.7.1.THE RISKS OF DOWNLOADING FREE ANTI-VIRUS SOFTWARE

It is very common for computer users to turn to **free anti-virus** software to protect their computer systems. While it is understandable that these people would opt for a free service, it is important to consider the potential negative consequences of using free anti-virus software and underestimating the risk involved.

• The main concern with using **free anti-virus** software is that it may offer **less protection** than paid-for anti-virus software. The free versions do not cover as many threats or benefit from the regular updates that are available in the paid versions. In some cases, free anti-virus software may be less effective at detecting and eliminating certain forms of **malware**.

For example, a free antivirus solution may not be able to detect, isolate and remove malicious software that is known to infect computer systems and cause problems.

- Another risk associated with using free anti-virus software is its ability to block certain websites or applications. Many paid-for anti-virus software packages offer more robust protection against malicious websites and allow users to control their settings to block certain types of content or activity. However, some **free antivirus** solutions may not be able to provide this level of protection and may even block legitimate websites or applications that are essential for web browsing.
- In addition, when a **system is infected** by **malware**, the free antivirus solution may not be able to provide detailed and comprehensive technical support. In this case, users should look to third-party services for advice on how to resolve the problem, or contact the manufacturer's technical support. However, most manufacturers only offer limited technical support to users who have purchased a paid version of the antivirus product.

. Finally, it's also worth mentioning that **free antivirus solutions** may not offer the same **quality of protection** as a paid version. Most paid-for antivirus software benefits from advanced technology that enables users to constantly monitor their online activities and quickly and easily clean the system of existing malware and potential threats.

Free anti-virus software generally lacks the advanced tools and high level of protection needed to give your system optimum protection against malware and other online **threats**.

In conclusion, it is important that users understand the **risks associated with** using a **free anti-virus** product compared with a paid-for product, so that they can make an informed decision about how they wish to protect their computer system.

Paid antivirus solutions offer more **robust** and **comprehensive** protection against all types of online threats, as well as additional features such as detailed and comprehensive technical support if required.

VI.8.INSTALLING AN ANTIVIRUS SOFTWARE

Installing an antivirus doesn't necessarily require you to be a computer expert. The free and paid software available in 2024 is designed to be intuitive and accessible to all Internet users. In fact, whether you're using a PC, MacOS or smartphone, it takes less than 6 minutes from download to installation of an antivirus.

To install an antivirus on Windows 10, here are the 5 steps to follow :

1. Create an account (depending on your antivirus software)

Some antivirus software on Windows 10 doesn't require you to register for the first few days of use. If this is the case, go straight to the second step at . Otherwise, first open your account by entering your personal details (address, surname, first name, telephone number, email address).

2. Download the antivirus

From the publisher's official website, all you have to do is click on the "Download" button and select "Download on Windows 10" from the list. The installation file will automatically start downloading. Allow just a few seconds (depending on your internet connection) to complete this second step.

3. Install Windows 10 antivirus

Depending on the software you downloaded, you may now find an .EXE or .ZIP file in your Windows 10 downloads. On an .EXE file, simply click on it to start the installation. On a .ZIP file, you'll need to right-click and then "Extract Files" to then launch your .EXE installation file. During this stage, make sure that your computer is plugged into the mains.

4. Configure the software

Throughout the installation process, the antivirus editor will ask you to customise the settings if you need to, and to make choices. This is when your validation key may be requested if you are paying for the antivirus. Don't forget to accept notifications from this software and also a launch each time Windows 10 starts up. If you need help at this point, Techopedia recommends contacting support for assistance.

5. Scan your system

Now you're all set to have your Windows 10 PC protected by a third-party antivirus. Simply open the installed application from your desktop and run an initial full scan of your computer. Depending on the software you've decided to install, this can take between a few minutes and a few hours. You can then schedule regular scans throughout the week.

INSTALLING ANTIVIRUS SOFTWARE ON WINDOWS 11

To install an antivirus on Windows 11, here are the 5 steps to follow :

1. Create an account (depending on your antivirus software)

In the same way, software available on Windows 11 can also be tested free of charge and without registration for a defined period (generally 30 days after installation). However, some solutions require you to register on the official website first. Follow the steps and complete the information requested before moving on to the second stage.

2. Download the antivirus

Taking care to check that you are on a reliable site from Windows 11 and that you are not on a malicious site (via a secure link from Techopedia), you now need to click on the "Download" tab and then select the file suitable for Windows 11. The installation file will automatically download to your computer.

3. Install Windows 11 antivirus

Once your download is complete, all you have to do is run your antivirus installation program. Techopedia recommends that you use the shortcut Ctrl + J to open the download window on Windows 11, then double-click on the previously downloaded file. The software will instantly launch on your PC.

4. Configure the software

All you have to do is follow the instructions that appear on your computer screen. Antivirus software can usually ask you about your habits on Windows 11 and the different configurations you want to use to protect yourself. If you have a paid subscription, you can enter the activation code at this stage of the installation.

5. Run an initial scan

Your antivirus now appears in the Windows 11 Welcome Centre and can be launched just like any other application. Click on it and run your first full system scan to get off to a good start with your new antivirus. It will detect, immobilise and annihilate malicious and large files that can slow down your PC.

V I.9. ARTIFICIAL INTELLIGENCE

Artificial intelligence (AI) is a process of imitating human intelligence, based on the creation and application of algorithms executed in a dynamic computer environment. Its aim is to enable computers to think and act like human beings.

VI.9.1. ARTIFICIAL/AUTOMATIC OR MACHINE LEARNING

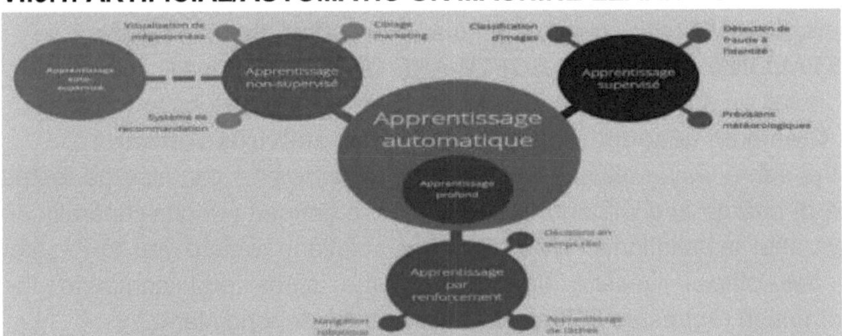

Machine Learning is a technique that involves training a computer to identify patterns, make predictions and learn from past experience without explicit programming.

V I.9.1.1.DIFFERENCE BETWEEN MACHINE LEARNING AND ARTIFICIAL INTELLIGENCE

Machine Learning (or AA) is a sub-category of Artificial Intelligence (AI) that uses algorithms to identify patterns and make predictions in a set of data. This can be numbers, text or even images. Under ideal conditions, machine learning enables human beings to interpret data faster and more accurately than they would be able to do themselves.

V I.9.1.2.HOW MACHINE LEARNING WORKS

Artificial intelligence is a form of virtual intelligence that resembles that of a human being, created by humans in a machine. In machine learning, machines are programmed to reproduce specific cognitive functions that are natural to humans, such as perception, learning and problem solving. For a machine to think like a human, it needs to be trained to create its own predictive model. This model enables the machine to analyse data in order to become a machine "capable of learning". To start this process, you need to provide the computer with data and choose a learning model to tell the machine how to process the data.

A machine learning model can use data to perform three actions:

- describe an event ;
- predicting an event ;

. make suggestions for future action.

The learning model chosen to train the machine depends on the complexity of the task and the desired result. There are three types of learning automatic :

Supervised learning: these models are trained using labelled data sets. They are used for tasks such as image recognition. **Unsupervised learning**: these models analyse unlabelled data to identify similarities, patterns and trends. They are used for tasks such as customer segmentation, recommendation systems and general data mining.

Reinforced learning: these models are trained using a trial-and-error process as part of an established reward system. They are used, for example, to train a computer to play a game in which actions lead to victory or defeat.

Once the computer has grasped how it should interpret the data (thanks to the learning model and the training data), it is able to make predictions and perform tasks when presented with new data. Its predictions become more accurate as it learns from continuous streams of data, and it becomes capable of performing tasks more quickly and accurately than a human could.

VI.9.1.3.AREAS OF APPLICATION

Machine learning and artificial intelligence technologies can be used to improve the user experience, anticipate customer behaviour and monitor systems to detect fraud. They can also help healthcare providers detect potentially fatal diseases. Machine learning is very much a part of our everyday lives:

- in the recommendation algorithms used by streaming services;
- in automatic switchboards and chatbots ;
- in target advertising ;
- in the automated quotes issued by financial institutions.

Generative AI, on which many AI tools are based today, exists thanks to deep learning, a machine learning technique used to analyse and interpret large quantities of data. Large Language Models (LLMs) are a sub set of generative AI. It is a crucial application of machine learning that demonstrates the ability to understand and generate human language on an unprecedented scale.

Machine learning is becoming a must-have feature for many businesses, and AI/AA applications are currently transforming the healthcare, financial services, telecommunications, utilities and many other sectors.

VI.9.2. BIG DATA AND NOSQL

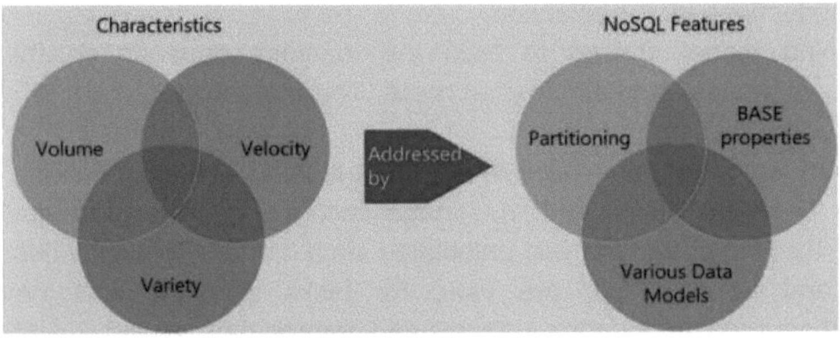

WHAT IS A NOSQL DATABASE?

There are two main ways of storing data. SQL (Structured Query Language) and NoSQL (*Not only SQL*). SQL is a computer language used to arrange data according to a precise schema and order. It allows data to be found and organised fairly quickly. NoSQL, as its name suggests, allows data to be stored without a precise schema, in a random, more flexible way. NoSQL is said to be "non-relational". It is best used for large databases (the famous Big Data). To put it simply, think of SQL as a library of highly organised books. The books are all arranged without leaving any room for chance (alphabetical order, by author, by theme, etc). This library also has members who can hire books. Depending on their age, for example, they will not have access to the adult section of the library. Also, a book cannot be hired at the same time by two members, and so on. This implies a number of constraints in terms of book storage and rental, which will disappear with NoSQL.

In fact, this much more recent language works without any storage constraints. In my NoSQL library, I can directly arrange a book without worrying about putting it on the right shelf, indicating a theme or assigning it an author. In other words, I can throw it into a pile of books without having to worry about distinguishing them from one another except by their title (the distribution key*). If a member of the library rents a book, I'll put a post-it note on the book indicating that it's being rented and by whom.

THE PROBLEM OF NOSQL FOR DATA ANALYSIS

First of all, there is a difference between storing data and analysing data. When it comes to storage, the usefulness of NoSQL is not in question. In fact, it's much quicker to store a book by tossing it into a stack (NoSQL) rather than looking for the right shelf, then indicating the theme, author, number of pages etc (SQL). What's more, the denormalisation* in our example consists of physically separating our single stack of books into several smaller stacks of books. In fact, it's much quicker to arrange your books in several smaller stacks of books with one person in charge per stack (NoSQL) rather than one person in charge of the whole library and all the books (SQL).

But when you want to analyse all your data, put them together and draw conclusions, that's when things get complicated.

If every month you have to carry out an inventory of your library, or carry out a study of rentals by theme or by member, you'll soon realise that the type of library is very important!

In the case of a SQL library, the inventory is very quick. The books are already sorted by subject and alphabetical order. Even before starting the analysis, you already have a large amount of information. For example, the sports bookshelf contains 70 books, 22 of which have been rented.

In the case of a NoSQL library, you risk pulling your hair out during the inventory. You have a pile of books, so the only way to carry out the inventory is to analyse each book, to read and analyse every possible post-it note you've added beforehand.

This difference in time, on an IT scale, is proportionally the same. When your library contains billions of books, and you have to make an inventory every day, or even every hour, the difference in time and therefore cost will be far from negligible.

VI.9.2.1.DEFINITION OF TERMS

SQL and NoSQL have already been explained at length in the article, but the first article still contains a few technical words.

Distribution key: this guarantees that the data is distributed across the different machines (in our example, the books) Denormalisation : this ensures that each line of the database contains all the data.

VI.9.3. CONNECTED OBJECTS AND IA

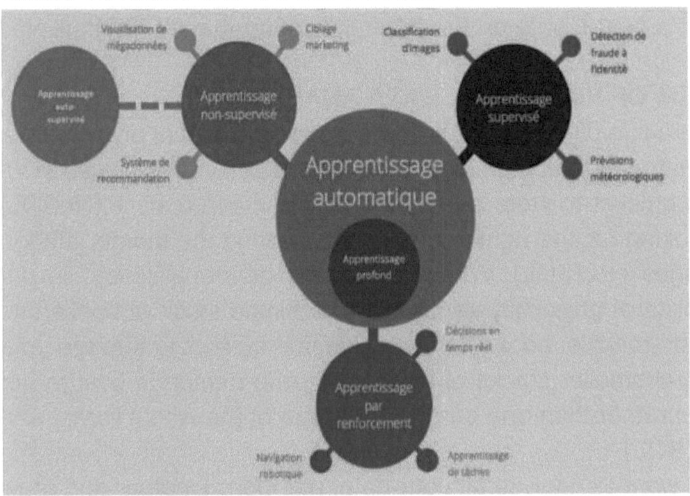

Since the 1990s, connected objects have become an increasingly common part of our daily lives.

From the development of their technical infrastructures, known as the "Internet of Things", to those of the "Internet of Everything Connected", technologies are now converging with artificial intelligence and Big Data towards an "Internet of Behaviour", where the challenge is now behavioural analysis. The number of connected objects sold could increase from 50 billion to 200 billion by 2025. These new devices, which can capture, analyse and display data in real time, are rapidly becoming part of every aspect of daily life.

VI.9.3.1.CONNECTED OBJECTS

Connected objects are everyday objects that are accessible to everyone, that can be controlled remotely via an application, and to which an internet connection is added, making them "connected".

This is why we distinguish between a connected object and a web access interface, although the latter can take the form of an everyday object.

OPERATION

Connected objects are linked to the Internet: they can therefore communicate with other systems to obtain or supply information, such as data marketing. This is made possible by the significant miniaturisation of electronic components, but also by the emergence of new telecommunication networks (see below). Connected objects will be able to :

+- collect and store data based on their environment: the user's heart rate, the humidity in a cellar, etc.

+ process data and information gathered from the web and the object's environment, then trigger actions accordingly, such as watering a lawn on the eve of a very dry day. ;

+- This is the case, for example, with connected glasses designed for the visually impaired or blind, which use cameras and facial recognition systems that analyse the surrounding environment to alert users to their surroundings. This information, translated into sound or speech, guides them along their route, identifying the people around them (if the people are already registered in the glasses' software).

VI.10. IA SEARCH ALGORITHMS

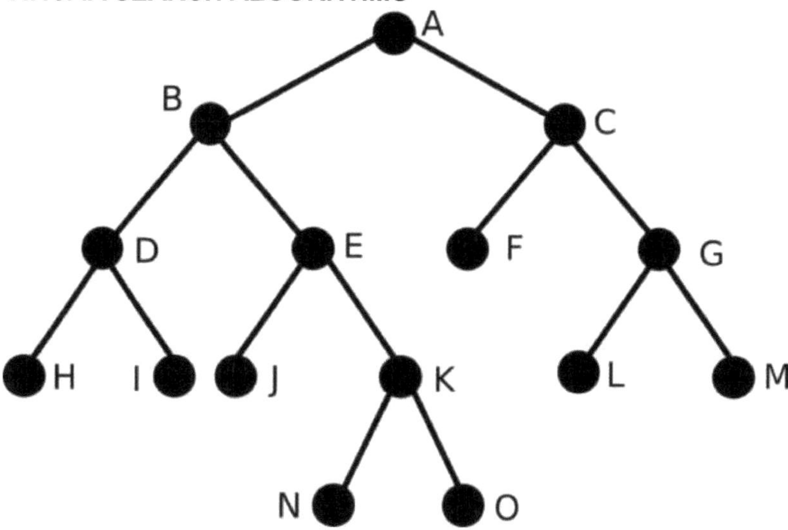

AI-powered search algorithms use machine learning to understand user intent and deliver relevant results. They analyse a variety of factors, including website content (text, images, videos, links), site structure (navigation, page hierarchy) and user behaviour (clicks, dwell time, bounce rate). These algorithms evolve over time, becoming more sophisticated.

VI.10.1.EXAMPLES OF IA SEARCH ALGORITHMS

Some examples of AI-powered search algorithms include:

. Google's **RankBrain**, which uses machine learning to understand user queries and deliver relevant results, processes around 15% of Google queries.

. **BERT**, also from Google, which improves natural language understanding for more accurate user queries and search results.

- **Passage Ranking**, another Google algorithm, identifies the most relevant passages in a document to improve the quality of search results, particularly for complex queries.

V I.10.2.EMERGING TRENDS IN IA SEARCH ALGORITHMS

Two emerging trends are influencing AI search algorithms:

. **Voice search**: Increasingly popular thanks to voice assistants such as Siri, Alexa and Google Assistant, voice search is understood by AI search engines thanks to machine learning.

. **Visual Search**: This trend allows users to search for information from images, with AI analysing these images to provide relevant results.

V I.10.3.THE IMPORTANCE OF ADAPTING TO CHANGE

Traditional SEO strategies, such as keyword stuffing and artificial link building, are no longer effective. AI search algorithms have become much more sophisticated at detecting these practices. SEO specialists need to adapt to AI search algorithms to maintain or improve the visibility of their websites.

V I.10.4.BEST PRACTICES FOR ADAPTING TO IA ALGORITHMS

To adapt to AI search algorithms, here are a few best practices:

- **Exploit the opportunities offered by AI**: Use AI as a tool to improve SEO by analysing data, optimising content, generating keywords, monitoring the competition, etc. Integrating AI on the site, such as chatbots, voice assistants and personalised recommendations, can also enrich user interaction.

. **Creating Quality Content**: Content remains the most crucial factor for SEO. AI search engines favour informative, well-structured and engaging content, providing users with relevant, useful and original information.

- **Use long-tail keywords**: Specific, less competitive keywords are easier to rank for and can generate more qualified traffic.
- **Optimising for Voice Search**: AI search engines are increasingly able to understand voice queries, requiring content to be optimised using natural language and simple phrases.

- **Respecting Search Intentions**: Creating content that responds specifically to different search intentions, whether to inform, buy or find local services.
- **Optimising for mobile devices**: With the majority of traffic coming from mobile devices, optimising for a smooth mobile experience is crucial.

• I.10.5. CHALLENGES AND OPPORTUNITIES FOR SEARCH ENGINE OPTIMISATION SPECIALISTS

The rise of AI search algorithms presents both challenges and opportunities for SEO specialists.

Challenge:

- AI search algorithms are becoming increasingly sophisticated and difficult to manipulate.
- SEO specialists have to adapt to the constant revolution in AI search algorithms.
- Creating high-quality, relevant content is more crucial than ever.

Opportunities :

- AI search algorithms deliver more relevant search results to users.
- SEO specialists can use these algorithms to gain a better understanding of users' intentions and create more effective content.
- AI search algorithms are opening up new opportunities, including optimisation for voice and visual search.

Conclusion

AI-powered search algorithms represent both a challenge and an opportunity for web professionals. To maintain the visibility of their websites and remain competitive, SEO specialists need to adapt to these algorithms by understanding how they work and adopting best practice. While keeping an eye on developments in the sector, the quality of content and the user experience remain at the heart of this adaptation.

V I.10.6. SEARCH ALGORITHM

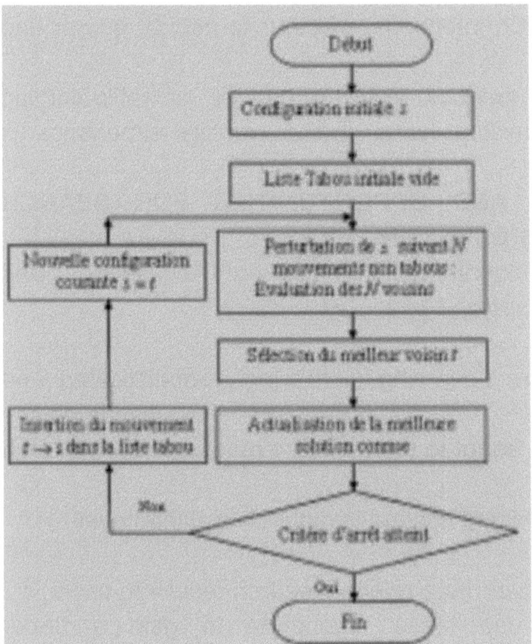

In computer science, a **search algorithm** is a type of algorithm which, for a given domain, a given problem and given criteria, returns a set of solutions to the problem.

Let's assume that the set of inputs is divisible into subsets, with respect to a given criterion, which could be, for example, an order relationship. In general, such an algorithm checks a certain number of these entries and returns one or more of the targeted entries as output.

The set of all potential solutions in the field is called the *search space*.

V I.10.6.1.CLASSICAL SEARCH ALGORITHMS

For common data structures such as lists, tables or trees, there are *well-known* algorithms that can be easily implemented in the same way as a recipe. These algorithms exploit the properties of the data structure and the domain.

A classic example is the dichotomous search, where the search space is divided in two at each attempt, giving logarithmic complexity (which is very advantageous).

V I.10.6.2.COMPLEXITY

These algorithms are at the centre of important questions in algorithmic complexity. They are also very important because of their wide range of applications.

Finding solutions to complex problems

For complex problems, finding solutions is a matter for artificial intelligence.

- An algorithm is said to be a brute force search when all the entries are checked one by one. This type of search can be effective if the solution space is of a reasonable size in relation to the power of the machine used to traverse it. It is therefore a method to be tried as a last resort if there is no other possibility.
- Heuristic search is used when additional knowledge or properties make the search more efficient. For example, using geometric symmetries to solve a puzzle can greatly reduce the *search space*. In the same way, a path search can be facilitated by even approximate knowledge of the direction in which the goal is located or its distance.

Examples

. Subchain search algorithm

. Pathfinding algorithm

VI.10.7. MINIMAX AND ALPHA-BETA ALGORITHM

A *two-player game* is classically defined as a tree whose nodes are *positions* (the root is called the "initial position of the game"). Each node is a "player" node (i.e. it is the player's turn to make a move) or an "opponent" node, and the players alternate, so that a player node has as its children a list of opponent nodes, obtained from the different moves available (symmetrically for opponent). If a node has no children, it is a terminal node, and in this case a *value* is associated with this node using a function *h*: *nodeterminal* -> **R** U {±infinite;} which indicates whether the player has won or lost. Typically, if we are only interested in games such as chess, we will have +infinity for winnings, -infinity for losses and 0 for the other positions (stalemates and other draws), but there are games with more complex evaluation structures, for example games where you bet money.

In a way, this tree contains all the possible games that can be played from the initial position. If we can explore the whole tree, we can determine whether there is a winning strategy for the player. If the tree is too big (or if time limits are imposed) we normally just explore the sub-tree obtained by truncating the game tree at a certain depth, and evaluating the truncated nodes using a heuristic *h'*.

In both cases, it is unreasonable to assume that the game tree is given extensively, and we prefer to present it implicitly by means of "game rules" which tell us how to obtain the list of children of a given position.

1. THE MINIMAX VISIT

The *MiniMax* algorithm, by Von Neumann, is very simple: we visit the game tree to bring up a value at the root (called the "game value") which is calculated recursively as follows:

. *MiniMax*(*p*)=*h*(*p*) if *p* is a terminal position

. *MiniMax*(*p*)=max(*MiniMax*(*o* 1), ..., *MiniMax*(o_n)) if *p* is a player position with children o1, ..., *then*

. *MiniMax*(*p*)=min(*MiniMax*(*j* 1), ..., *MiniMax*(j_m)) if *p* is an opposing position with children j1, ..., *jm*

We can check that *MiniMax*(*p*) is the best possible value from position *p*, if the opponent plays optimally. Clearly, to apply the MiniMax algorithm, all you need is

. a type of *position* data that represents the possible states of the game (and an initial position);

. a function *h* : *position* -> **R** U {±infinite} to evaluate terminal positions;

. a function *estjoueur* : *position* -> *{yes*, *no}* which is used to determine whether a position is a player or opponent position;

. an *accessible* function which takes a position *p* and returns the list of positions accessible by the moves available from *p*.

This gives us our C interface:

```
/* positions /*
/*
struct position {
. . . /* This depends on the game
.   and must not be used for tree visits */
};*/
typedef struct position *position;
/* a list of positions */
typedef struct {
int number;
position *table;
/* We use an array, the number of elements of which is above */
/* The moves to be played are represented by their position in the table.
*/
} posliste;
/* finally, the game's own functions */
double h(position p);
int isplayer(position p);
```

accessible poslist(position p);
*/ void libere(posliste pl);

2. THE ALPHA-BETA TOUR

The alpha-beta algorithm is an optimisation of MiniMax, which "cuts" subtrees as soon as their value becomes uninteresting for the purposes of calculating the MiniMax value of the game. So, on each node, in addition to the value, we'll be looking at two other quantities, called alpha and beta, which will be used to calculate the value of the node.

ALPHA OF A NODE

Is an approximation from below of the true value of the node. It is equal to the value on the leaves, and is initialized to -infinity elsewhere. Then, on the player nodes, it is kept equal to the largest value obtained on the children visited so far, and is equal to the alpha value of its predecessor on the opposite nodes.

BETA OF A N&UD

Is an approximation from above of the true value of the node. It is equal to the value on the leaves, and is initialized to +infinity elsewhere. Then, on the opposing nodes it is kept equal to the smallest value obtained on the children visited so far, and is equal to the beta value of its predecessor on the player nodes.

The ALPHA-BETA algorithm can be described by the following pseudo-code: function ALPHA-BETA(P, A, B) /* here A is always less than B */
if P is a leaf then
return the value of P otherwise
initialise Alpha of P a -infinite and Beta of P a +infinite
if P is a Min node then
for all children Pi of P do
Val = ALPHA-BETA(Pi, A, Min(B,Beta de P))
Beta of P = Min(Beta of P, Val)
If A >= Beta of P /*this is the alpha cut-off */
then return Beta of P finfaire
return Beta from P
or
for all children Pi of P do
Val = ALPHA-BETA(Pi, Max(A,Alpha de P), B)
Alpha of P = Max(Alpha of P, Val)
If Alpha of P >= B /*this is the beta cut-off */
then return Alpha from P
finfaire

return Alpha from P

We know that the true MiniMax value *v* of a node is framed by alpha and beta (i.e. alpha <= *v* <= beta), and if we call the ALPHA-BETA function with the values (*P*,-infini,+infini) we obtain exactly MiniMax(P). ALPHA-BETA can often be used to double the depth of exploration of a resource parity tree, compared with MiniMax.

MULTIPLE PROGRAMMING

If you have to manage a fairly large project, it is essential to be able to break it down into sub-projects with clearly specified interfaces, so that the various components can be developed in parallel while guaranteeing the coherence of the final result.

VI.10.8. STRENGTHS AND WEAKNESSES OF THE ALPHABETA SEARCH ALGORITHM

The advantage of the Alpha-beta algorithm lies in the fact that it eliminates from the search all the sub-trees which can be seen directly to make no contribution to the final value, and as a weakness lacking in strategy.

BIBLIOGRAPHY

- **The works**
- Guide to support the Science Learning Area Educational Programme, 2021 edition.
- Guillaume PLOUIN, *Cloud computing. Securite, gouvernance du SI hybride et panorama du marché,* 4e edition, Dunod, Paris, 2016.
- Jacques LONCHAMP, introduction aux systemes informatiques, Paris, Dunod, 2017.
- Claude Servin, *Reseaux et Telecoms, Cours et exercices corriges*, Paris, Dunod, 2003.
- Guy Pujolle, *Initiation aux reseaux*, cours et exercices, Paris, Eyrolles, 2001.
- **The websites :**
- https://mspoweruser.com
- https://www.inmac-wstore.com
- https://aws.amazon.com
- https://www.phpeasydata.com
- https://www.codyx.org
- https://commentouvrir.com
- https://web.maths.unsw.edu.au
- http://www.saveho.com,

Printed by Books on Demand GmbH, Norderstedt / Germany